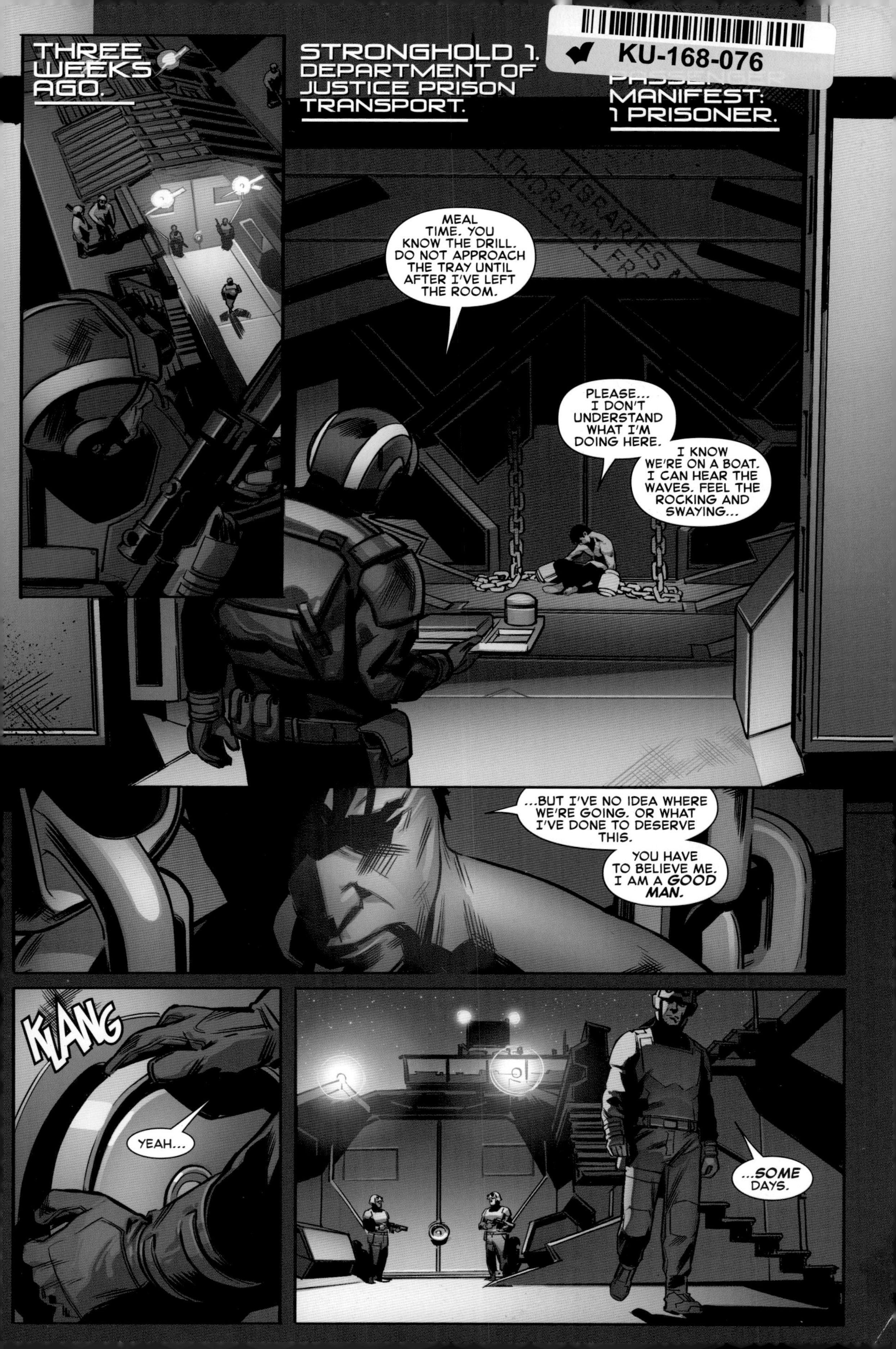
THREE WEEKS AGO.
STRONGHOLD 1. DEPARTMENT OF JUSTICE PRISON TRANSPORT.
MANIFEST: 1 PRISONER.
MEAL TIME. YOU KNOW THE DRILL. DO NOT APPROACH THE TRAY UNTIL AFTER I'VE LEFT THE ROOM.
PLEASE... I DON'T UNDERSTAND WHAT I'M DOING HERE.
I KNOW WE'RE ON A BOAT. I CAN HEAR THE WAVES. FEEL THE ROCKING AND SWAYING...
...BUT I'VE NO IDEA WHERE WE'RE GOING. OR WHAT I'VE DONE TO DESERVE THIS.
YOU HAVE TO BELIEVE ME. I AM A *GOOD MAN.*
KLANG
YEAH...
...*SOME* DAYS.

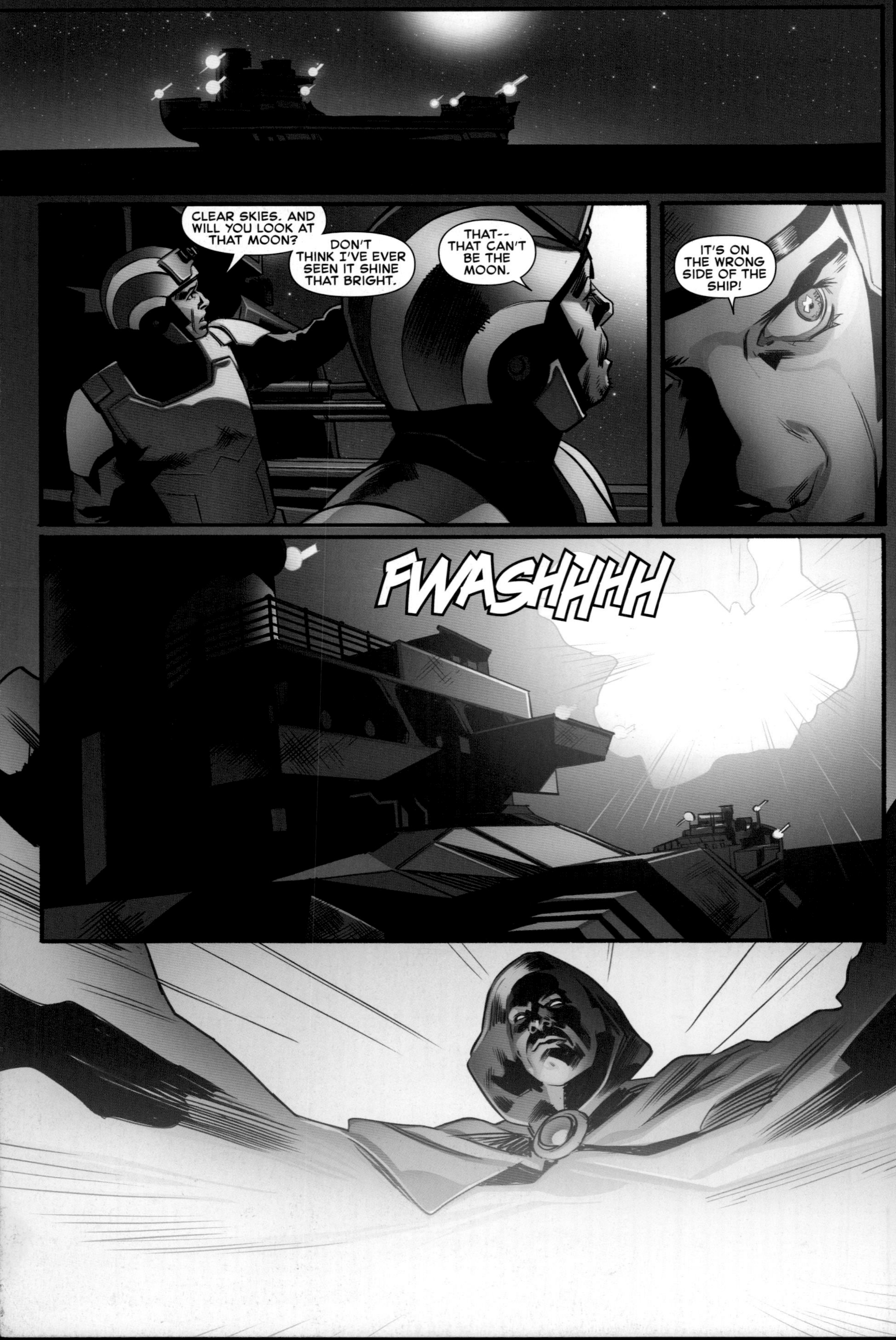
CLEAR SKIES. AND WILL YOU LOOK AT THAT MOON?
DON'T THINK I'VE EVER SEEN IT SHINE THAT BRIGHT.
THAT-- THAT CAN'T BE THE MOON.
IT'S ON THE WRONG SIDE OF THE SHIP!
FWASHHHH

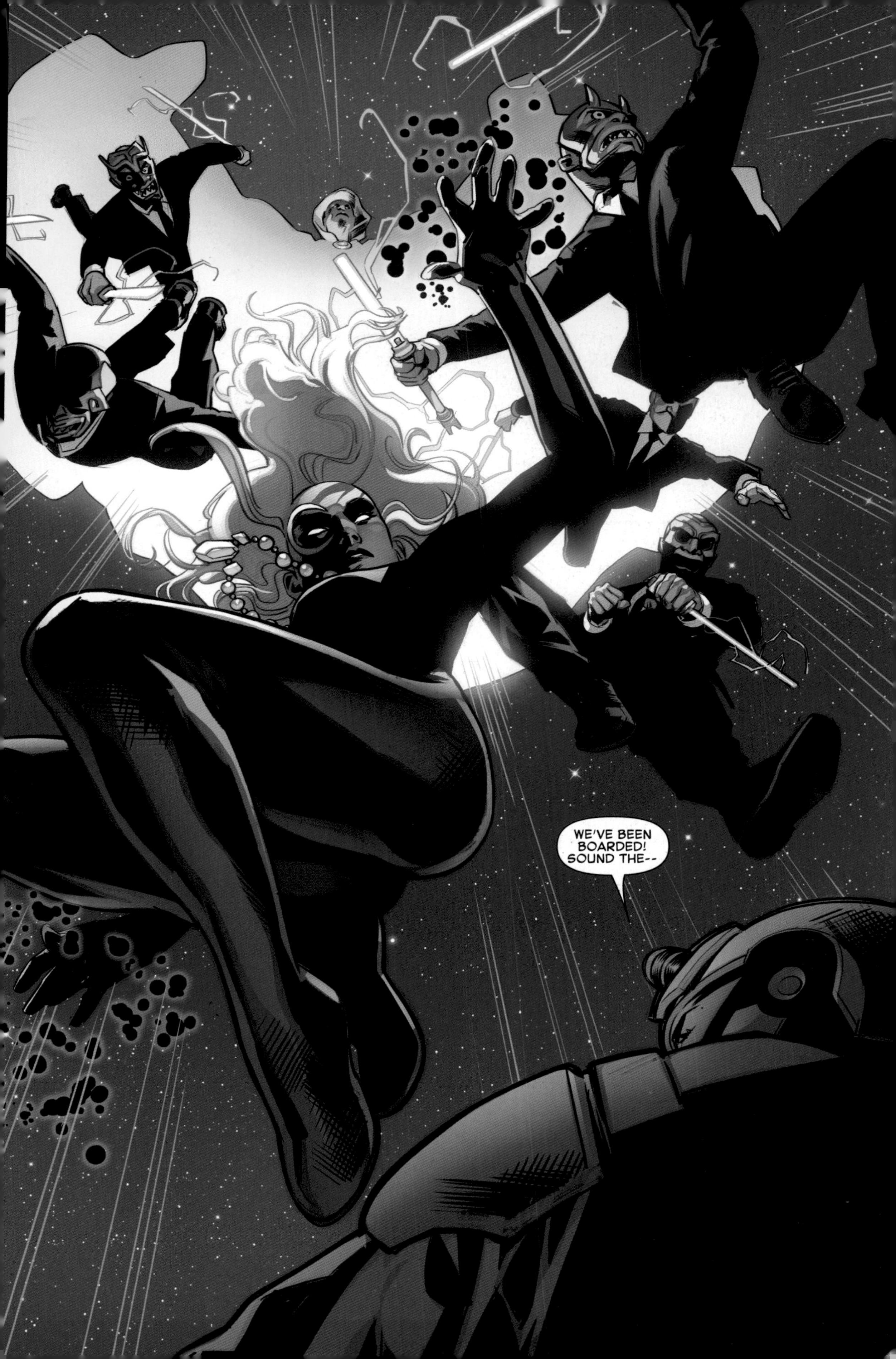
WE'VE BEEN BOARDED! SOUND THE--

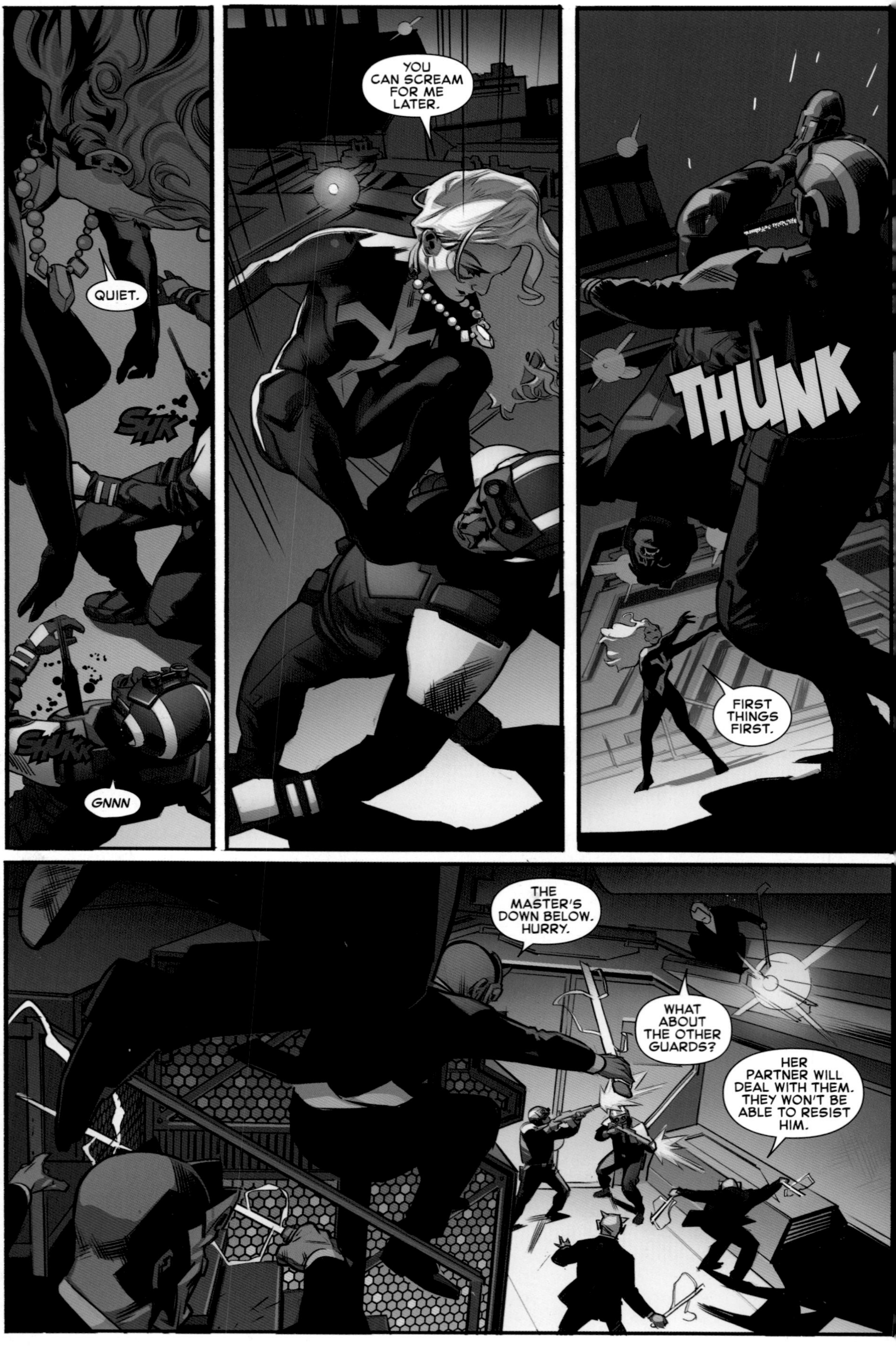
QUIET.
SHK
SHUKK
GNNN
YOU CAN SCREAM FOR ME LATER.
THUNK
FIRST THINGS FIRST.
THE MASTER'S DOWN BELOW. HURRY.
WHAT ABOUT THE OTHER GUARDS?
HER PARTNER WILL DEAL WITH THEM. THEY WON'T BE ABLE TO RESIST HIM.

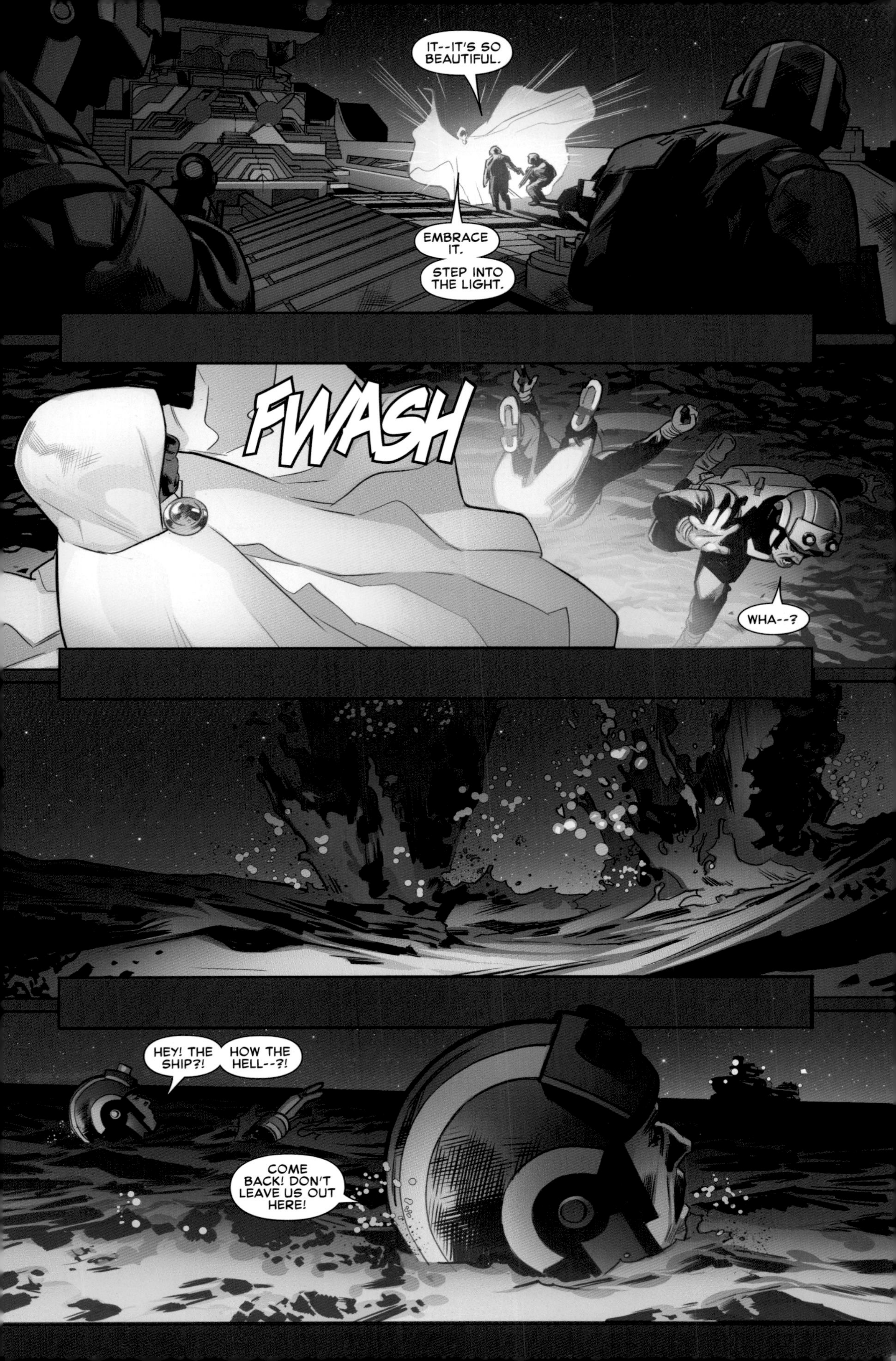
IT--IT'S SO BEAUTIFUL.
EMBRACE IT.
STEP INTO THE LIGHT.
FWASH
WHA--?
HEY! THE SHIP?!
HOW THE HELL--?!
COME BACK! DON'T LEAVE US OUT HERE!

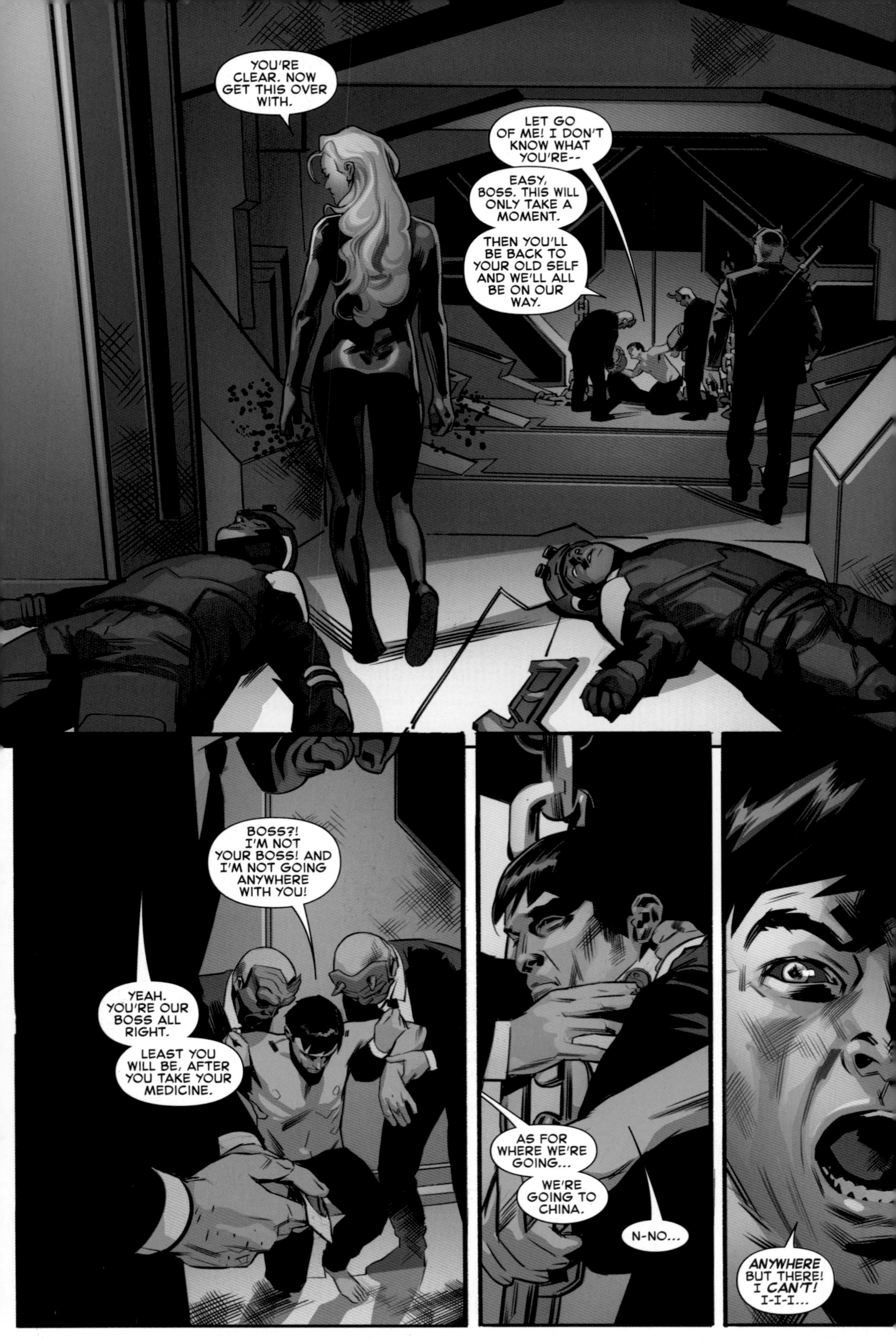

YOU'RE CLEAR. NOW GET THIS OVER WITH.
LET GO OF ME! I DON'T KNOW WHAT YOU'RE--
EASY, BOSS. THIS WILL ONLY TAKE A MOMENT.
THEN YOU'LL BE BACK TO YOUR OLD SELF AND WE'LL ALL BE ON OUR WAY.
BOSS?! I'M NOT YOUR BOSS! AND I'M NOT GOING ANYWHERE WITH YOU!
YEAH. YOU'RE OUR BOSS ALL RIGHT.
LEAST YOU WILL BE, AFTER YOU TAKE YOUR MEDICINE.
AS FOR WHERE WE'RE GOING...
WE'RE GOING TO CHINA.
N-NO...
ANYWHERE BUT THERE! I *CAN'T!* I-I-I...

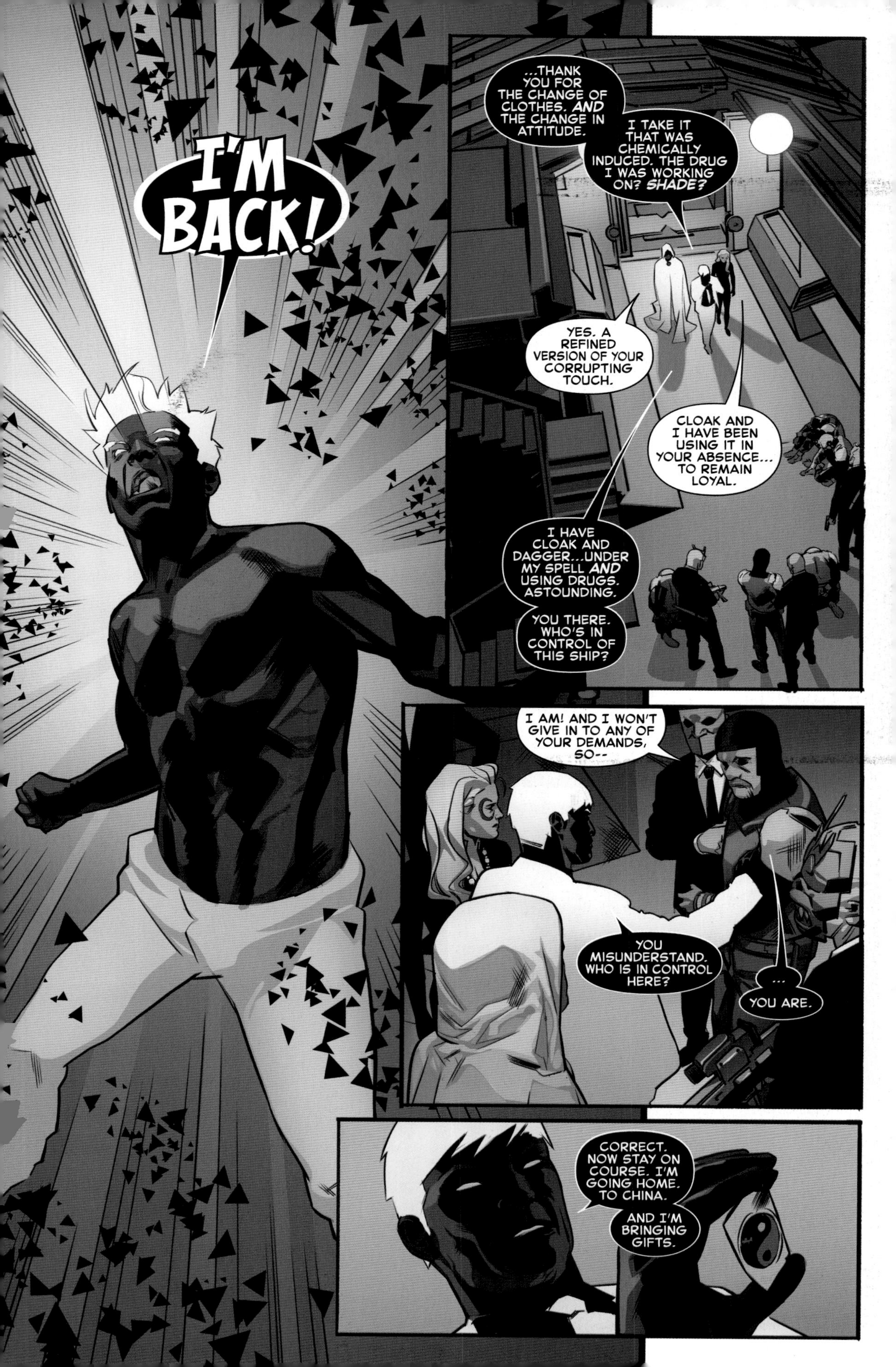
I'M BACK!
...THANK YOU FOR THE CHANGE OF CLOTHES. *AND* THE CHANGE IN ATTITUDE.
I TAKE IT THAT WAS CHEMICALLY INDUCED. THE DRUG I WAS WORKING ON? *SHADE?*
YES. A REFINED VERSION OF YOUR CORRUPTING TOUCH.
CLOAK AND I HAVE BEEN USING IT IN YOUR ABSENCE... TO REMAIN LOYAL.
I HAVE CLOAK AND DAGGER...UNDER MY SPELL *AND* USING DRUGS. ASTOUNDING.
YOU THERE. WHO'S IN CONTROL OF THIS SHIP?
I AM! AND I WON'T GIVE IN TO ANY OF YOUR DEMANDS, SO--
YOU MISUNDERSTAND. WHO IS IN CONTROL HERE?
...
YOU ARE.
CORRECT. NOW STAY ON COURSE. I'M GOING HOME. TO CHINA.
AND I'M BRINGING GIFTS.

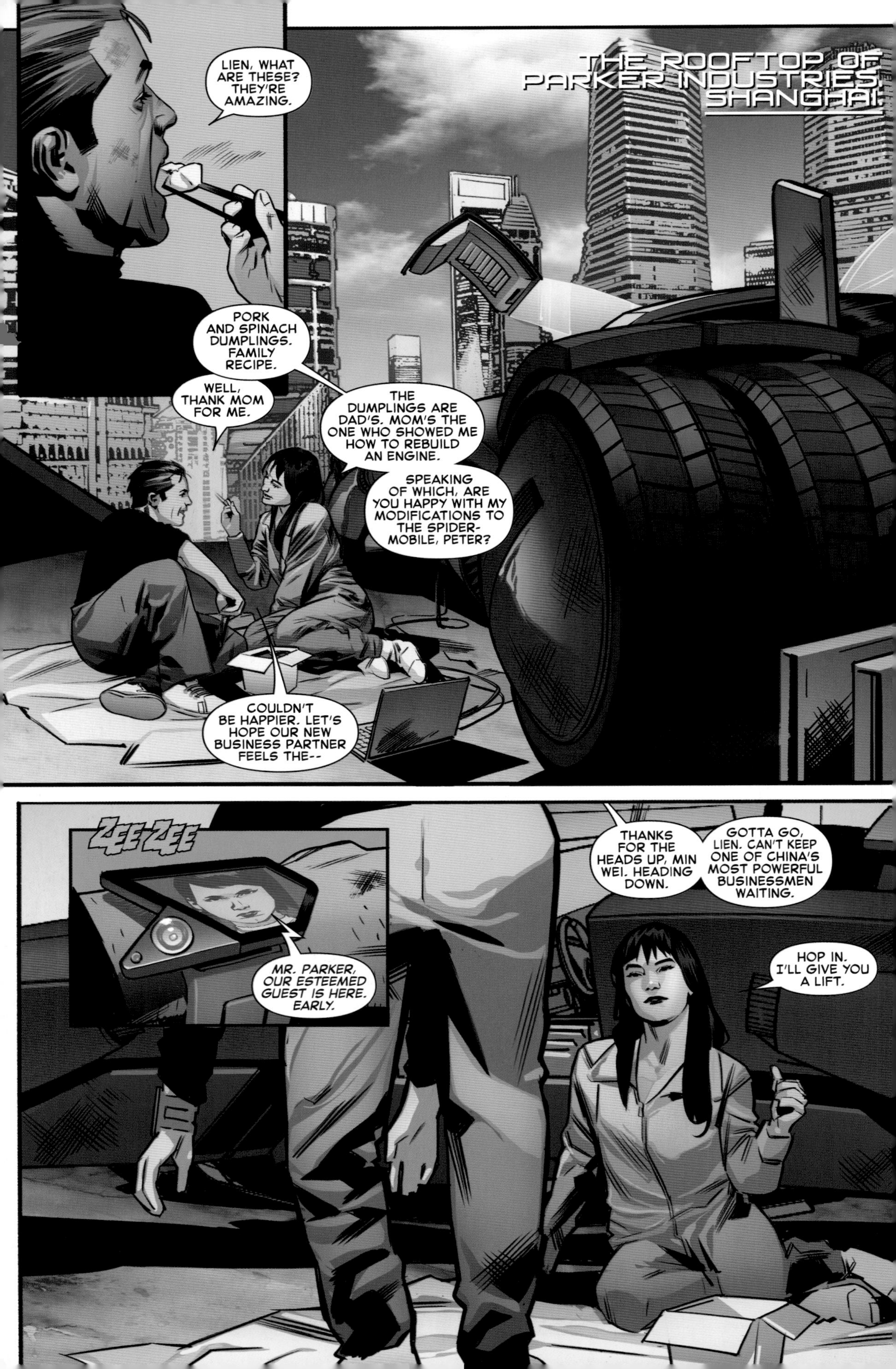
THE ROOFTOP OF PARKER INDUSTRIES, SHANGHAI.
LIEN, WHAT ARE THESE? THEY'RE AMAZING.
PORK AND SPINACH DUMPLINGS. FAMILY RECIPE.
WELL, THANK MOM FOR ME.
THE DUMPLINGS ARE DAD'S. MOM'S THE ONE WHO SHOWED ME HOW TO REBUILD AN ENGINE.
SPEAKING OF WHICH, ARE YOU HAPPY WITH MY MODIFICATIONS TO THE SPIDER-MOBILE, PETER?
COULDN'T BE HAPPIER. LET'S HOPE OUR NEW BUSINESS PARTNER FEELS THE--
ZEE ZEE
MR. PARKER, OUR ESTEEMED GUEST IS HERE. EARLY.
THANKS FOR THE HEADS UP, MIN WEI. HEADING DOWN.
GOTTA GO, LIEN. CAN'T KEEP ONE OF CHINA'S MOST POWERFUL BUSINESSMEN WAITING.
HOP IN. I'LL GIVE YOU A LIFT.

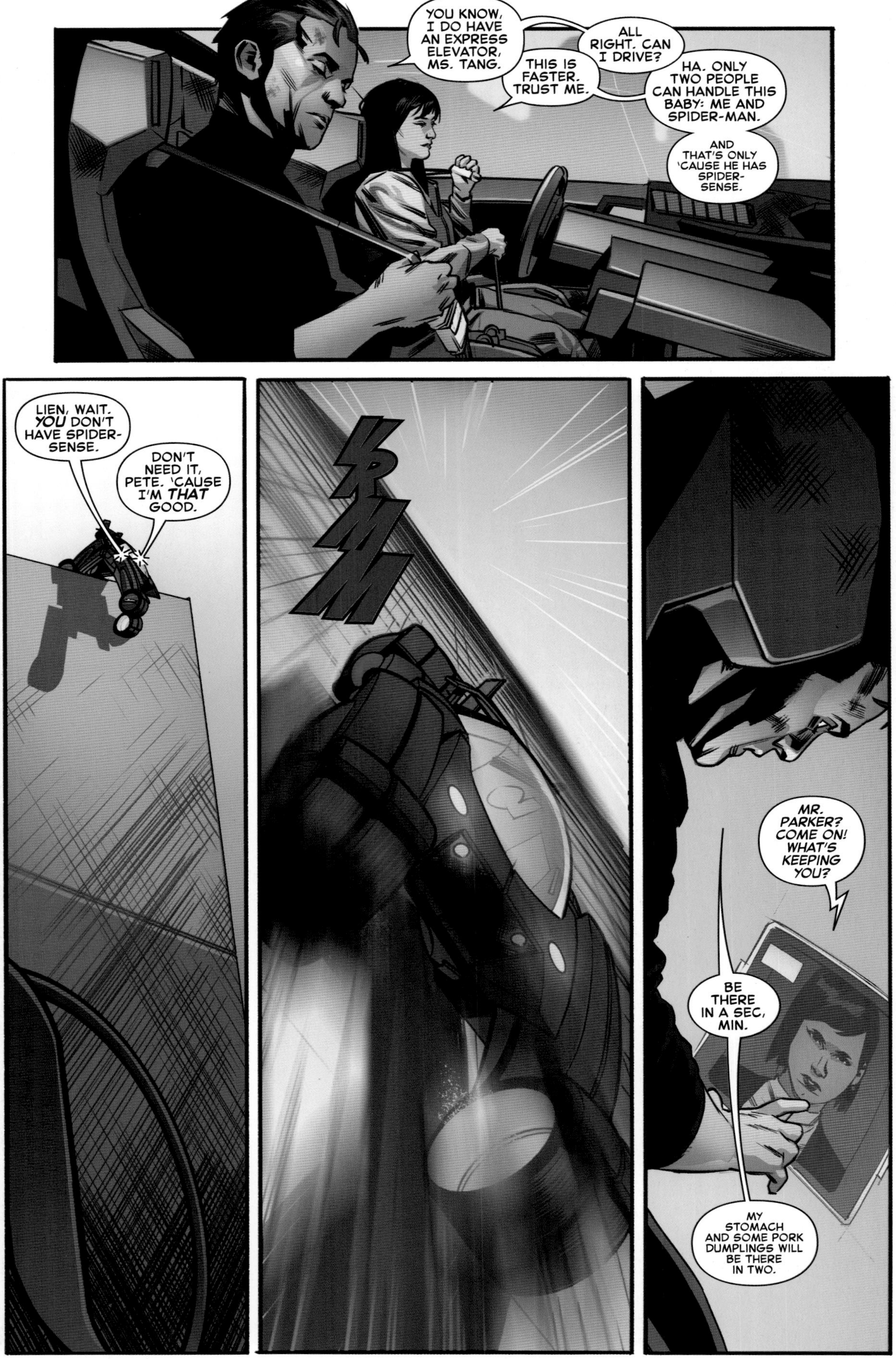
YOU KNOW, I DO HAVE AN EXPRESS ELEVATOR, MS. TANG.
THIS IS FASTER. TRUST ME.
ALL RIGHT. CAN I DRIVE?
HA. ONLY TWO PEOPLE CAN HANDLE THIS BABY: ME AND SPIDER-MAN.
AND THAT'S ONLY 'CAUSE HE HAS SPIDER-SENSE.
LIEN, WAIT. *YOU* DON'T HAVE SPIDER-SENSE.
DON'T NEED IT, PETE. 'CAUSE I'M *THAT* GOOD.
VRMM
MR. PARKER? COME ON! WHAT'S KEEPING YOU?
BE THERE IN A SEC, MIN.
MY STOMACH AND SOME PORK DUMPLINGS WILL BE THERE IN TWO.

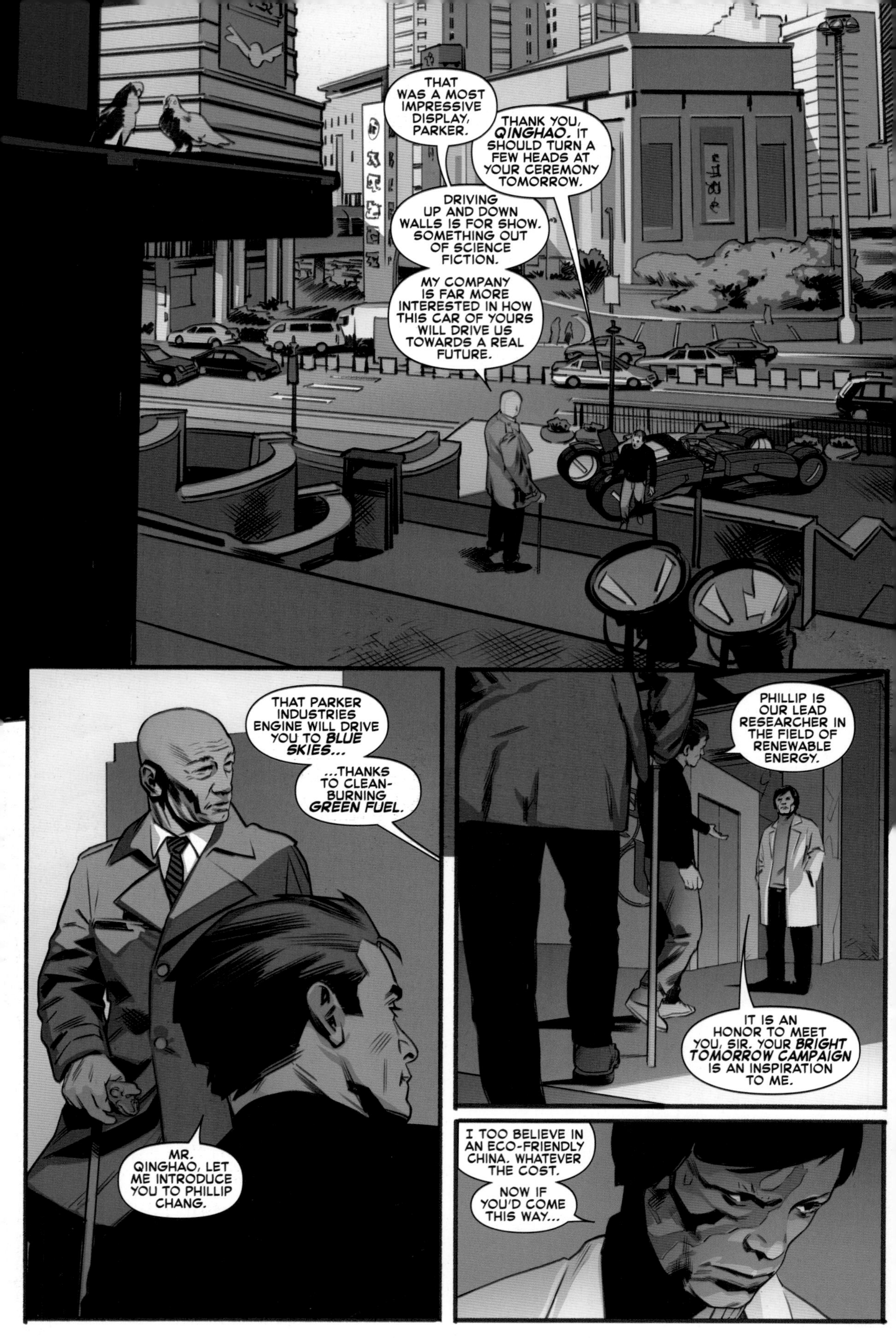
THAT WAS A MOST IMPRESSIVE DISPLAY, PARKER.
THANK YOU, QINGHAO. IT SHOULD TURN A FEW HEADS AT YOUR CEREMONY TOMORROW.
DRIVING UP AND DOWN WALLS IS FOR SHOW. SOMETHING OUT OF SCIENCE FICTION.
MY COMPANY IS FAR MORE INTERESTED IN HOW THIS CAR OF YOURS WILL DRIVE US TOWARDS A REAL FUTURE.
THAT PARKER INDUSTRIES ENGINE WILL DRIVE YOU TO BLUE SKIES...
...THANKS TO CLEAN-BURNING GREEN FUEL.
MR. QINGHAO, LET ME INTRODUCE YOU TO PHILLIP CHANG.
PHILLIP IS OUR LEAD RESEARCHER IN THE FIELD OF RENEWABLE ENERGY.
IT IS AN HONOR TO MEET YOU, SIR. YOUR BRIGHT TOMORROW CAMPAIGN IS AN INSPIRATION TO ME.
I TOO BELIEVE IN AN ECO-FRIENDLY CHINA. WHATEVER THE COST.
NOW IF YOU'D COME THIS WAY...

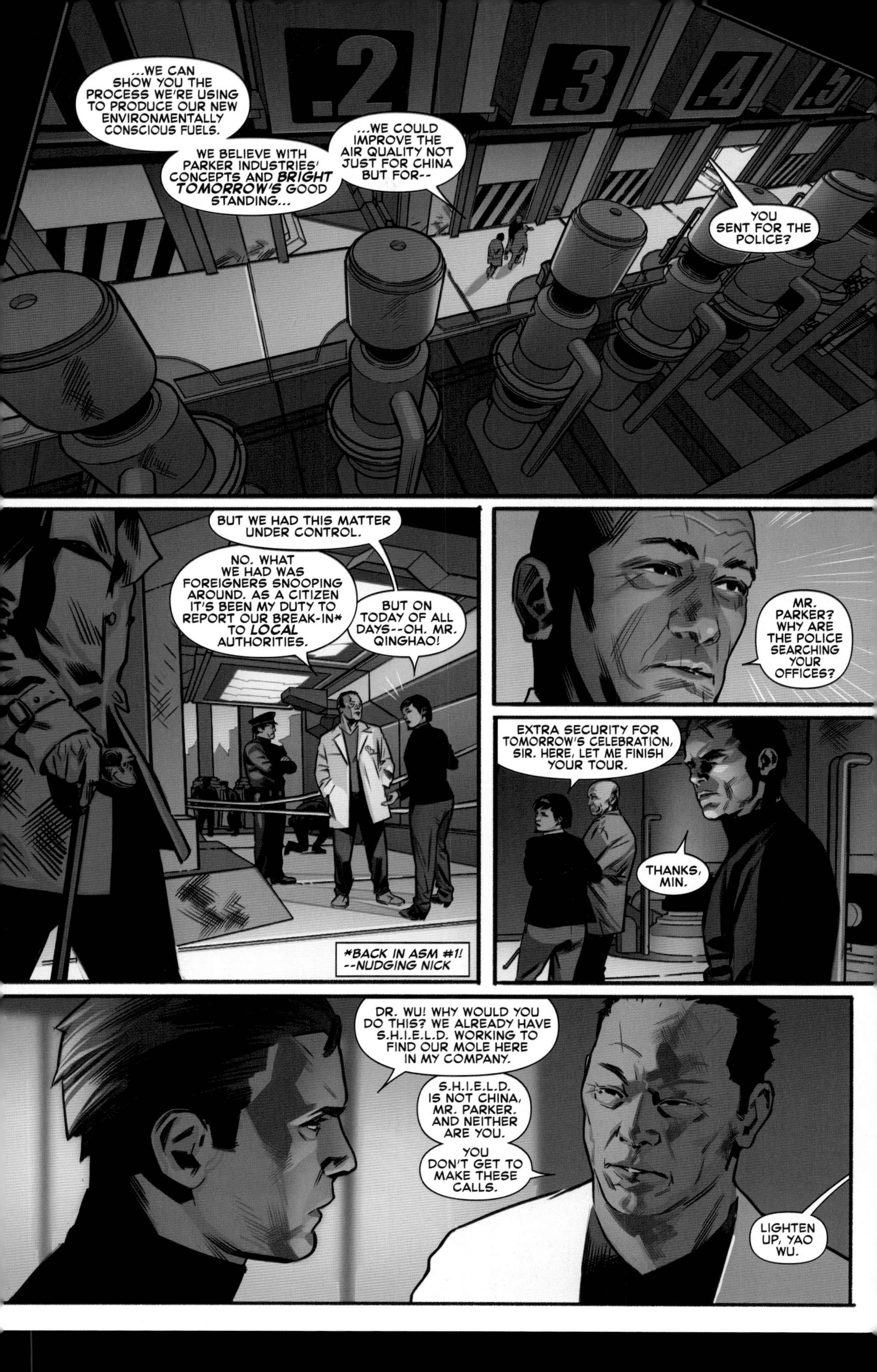
...WE CAN SHOW YOU THE PROCESS WE'RE USING TO PRODUCE OUR NEW ENVIRONMENTALLY CONSCIOUS FUELS.
WE BELIEVE WITH PARKER INDUSTRIES' CONCEPTS AND *BRIGHT TOMORROW'S* GOOD STANDING...
...WE COULD IMPROVE THE AIR QUALITY NOT JUST FOR CHINA BUT FOR--
YOU SENT FOR THE POLICE?
BUT WE HAD THIS MATTER UNDER CONTROL.
NO. WHAT WE HAD WAS FOREIGNERS SNOOPING AROUND. AS A CITIZEN IT'S BEEN MY DUTY TO REPORT OUR BREAK-IN* TO *LOCAL* AUTHORITIES.
BUT ON TODAY OF ALL DAYS--OH. MR. QINGHAO!
*BACK IN ASM #1! --NUDGING NICK
MR. PARKER? WHY ARE THE POLICE SEARCHING YOUR OFFICES?
EXTRA SECURITY FOR TOMORROW'S CELEBRATION, SIR. HERE, LET ME FINISH YOUR TOUR.
THANKS, MIN.
DR. WU! WHY WOULD YOU DO THIS? WE ALREADY HAVE S.H.I.E.L.D. WORKING TO FIND OUR MOLE HERE IN MY COMPANY.
S.H.I.E.L.D. IS NOT CHINA, MR. PARKER. AND NEITHER ARE YOU.
YOU DON'T GET TO MAKE THESE CALLS.
LIGHTEN UP, YAO WU.

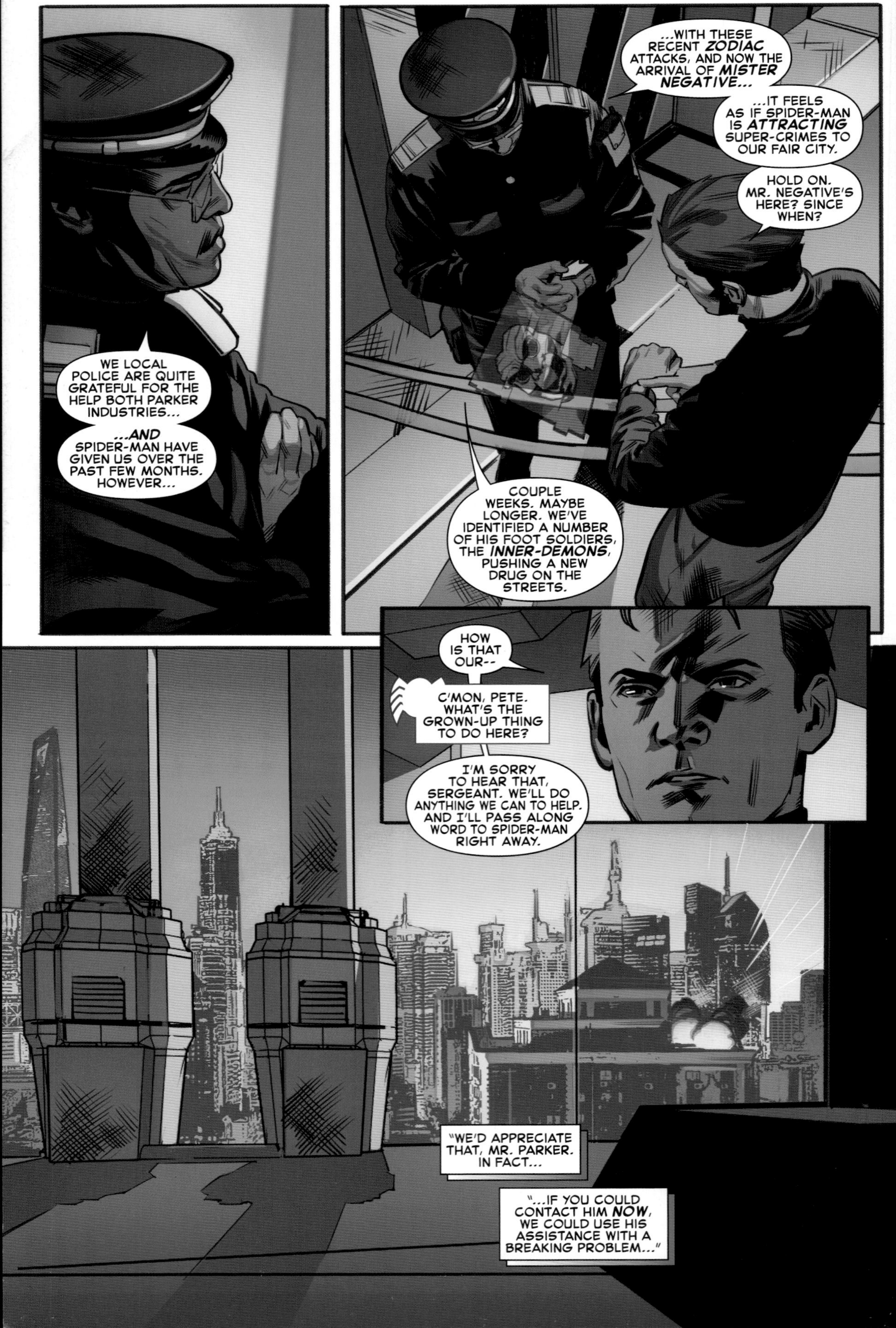
WE LOCAL POLICE ARE QUITE GRATEFUL FOR THE HELP BOTH PARKER INDUSTRIES...
...AND SPIDER-MAN HAVE GIVEN US OVER THE PAST FEW MONTHS. HOWEVER...
...WITH THESE RECENT ZODIAC ATTACKS, AND NOW THE ARRIVAL OF MISTER NEGATIVE...
...IT FEELS AS IF SPIDER-MAN IS ATTRACTING SUPER-CRIMES TO OUR FAIR CITY.
HOLD ON. MR. NEGATIVE'S HERE? SINCE WHEN?
COUPLE WEEKS. MAYBE LONGER. WE'VE IDENTIFIED A NUMBER OF HIS FOOT SOLDIERS, THE INNER-DEMONS, PUSHING A NEW DRUG ON THE STREETS.
HOW IS THAT OUR--
C'MON, PETE. WHAT'S THE GROWN-UP THING TO DO HERE?
I'M SORRY TO HEAR THAT, SERGEANT. WE'LL DO ANYTHING WE CAN TO HELP. AND I'LL PASS ALONG WORD TO SPIDER-MAN RIGHT AWAY.
"WE'D APPRECIATE THAT, MR. PARKER. IN FACT...
"...IF YOU COULD CONTACT HIM NOW, WE COULD USE HIS ASSISTANCE WITH A BREAKING PROBLEM..."

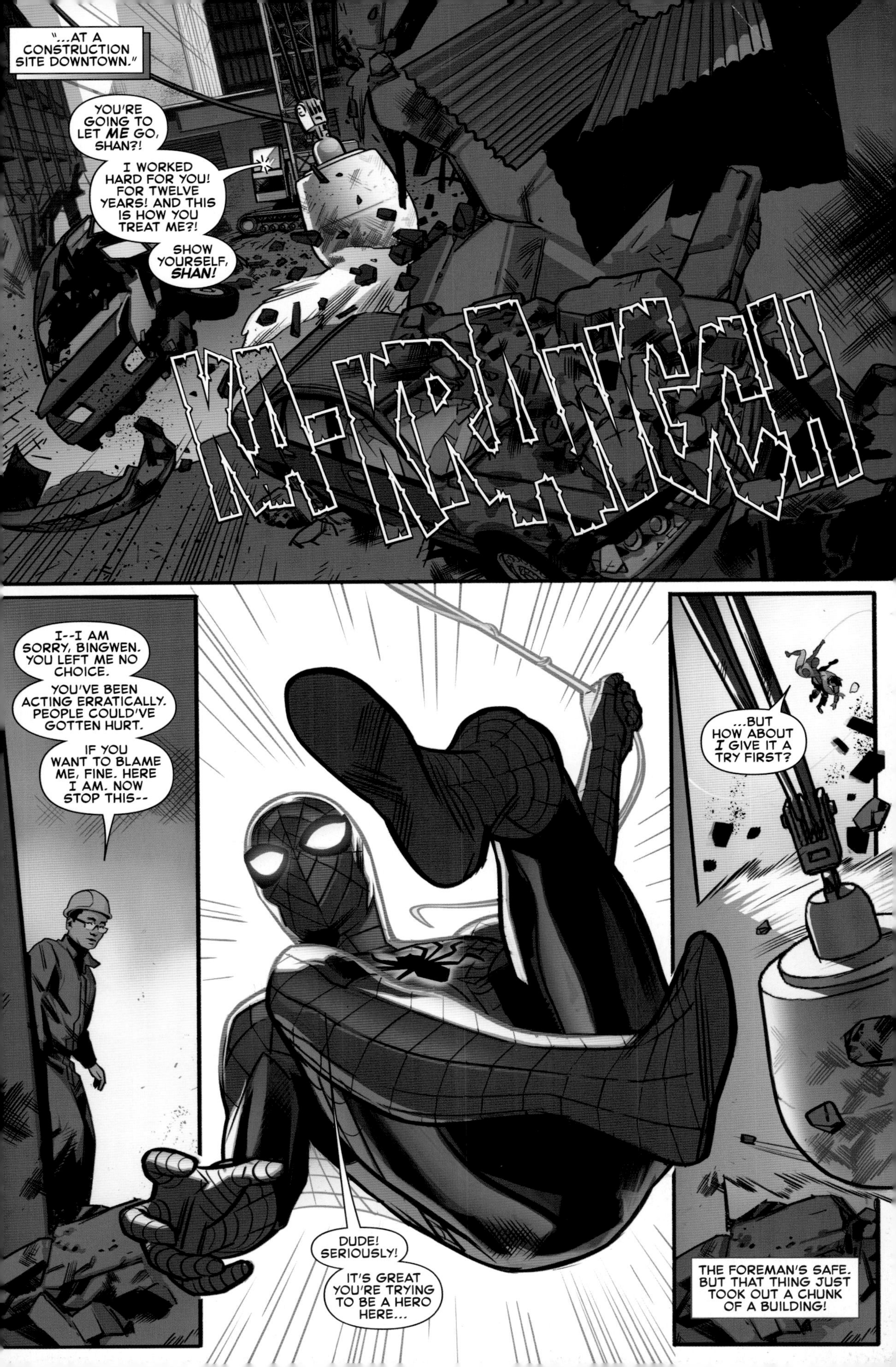

"...AT A CONSTRUCTION SITE DOWNTOWN."
YOU'RE GOING TO LET *ME* GO, SHAN?!
I WORKED HARD FOR YOU! FOR TWELVE YEARS! AND THIS IS HOW YOU TREAT ME?!
SHOW YOURSELF, ***SHAN!***
KA-KRAKNGCH
I--I AM SORRY, BINGWEN. YOU LEFT ME NO CHOICE.
YOU'VE BEEN ACTING ERRATICALLY. PEOPLE COULD'VE GOTTEN HURT.
IF YOU WANT TO BLAME ME, FINE. HERE I AM. NOW STOP THIS--
DUDE! SERIOUSLY!
IT'S GREAT YOU'RE TRYING TO BE A HERO HERE...
...BUT HOW ABOUT *I* GIVE IT A TRY FIRST?
THE FOREMAN'S SAFE. BUT THAT THING JUST TOOK OUT A CHUNK OF A BUILDING!

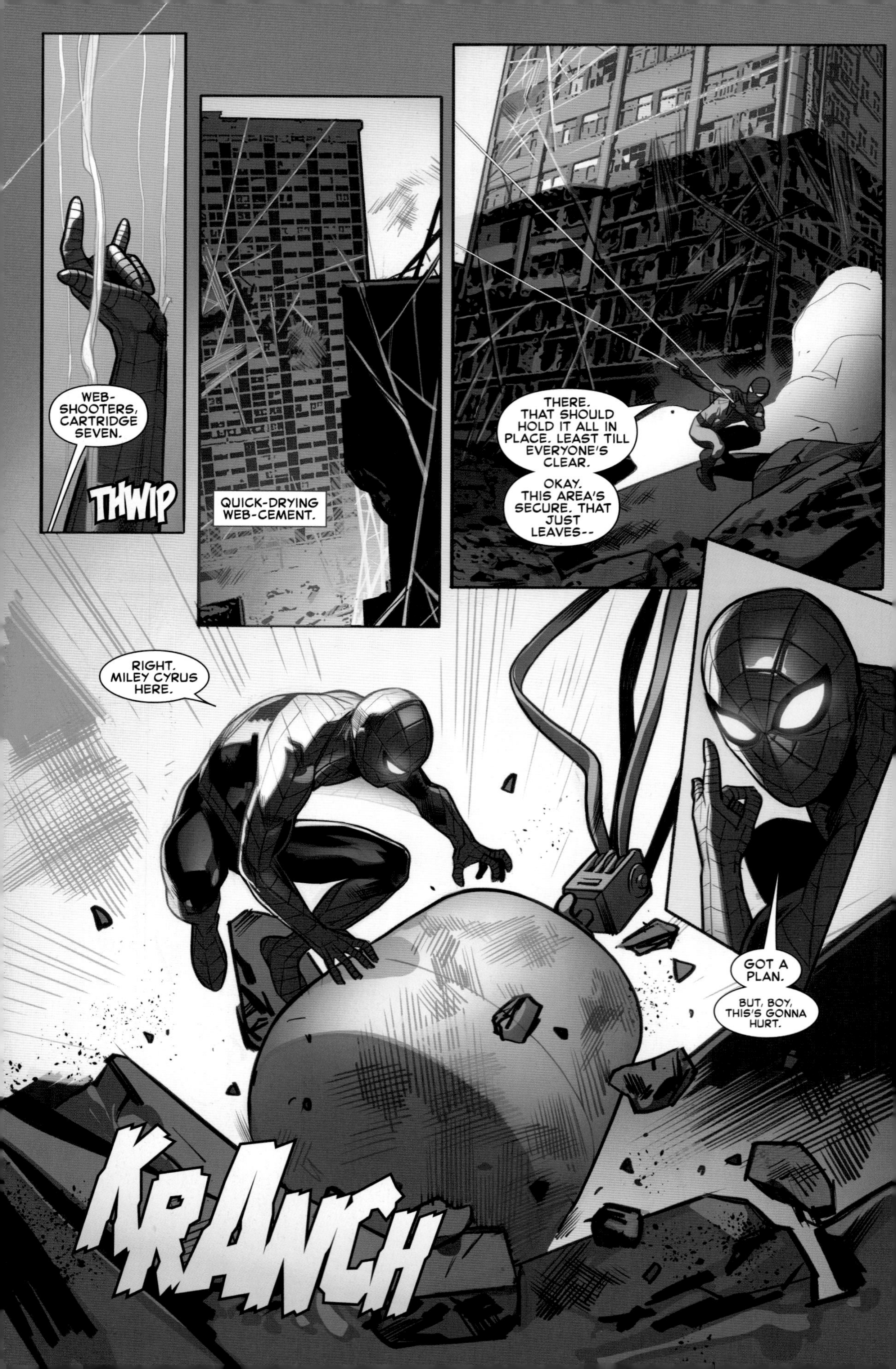
WEB-SHOOTERS, CARTRIDGE SEVEN.
THWIP
QUICK-DRYING WEB-CEMENT.
THERE. THAT SHOULD HOLD IT ALL IN PLACE. LEAST TILL EVERYONE'S CLEAR.
OKAY. THIS AREA'S SECURE. THAT JUST LEAVES--
RIGHT. MILEY CYRUS HERE.
GOT A PLAN.
BUT, BOY, THIS'S GONNA HURT.
KRANCH

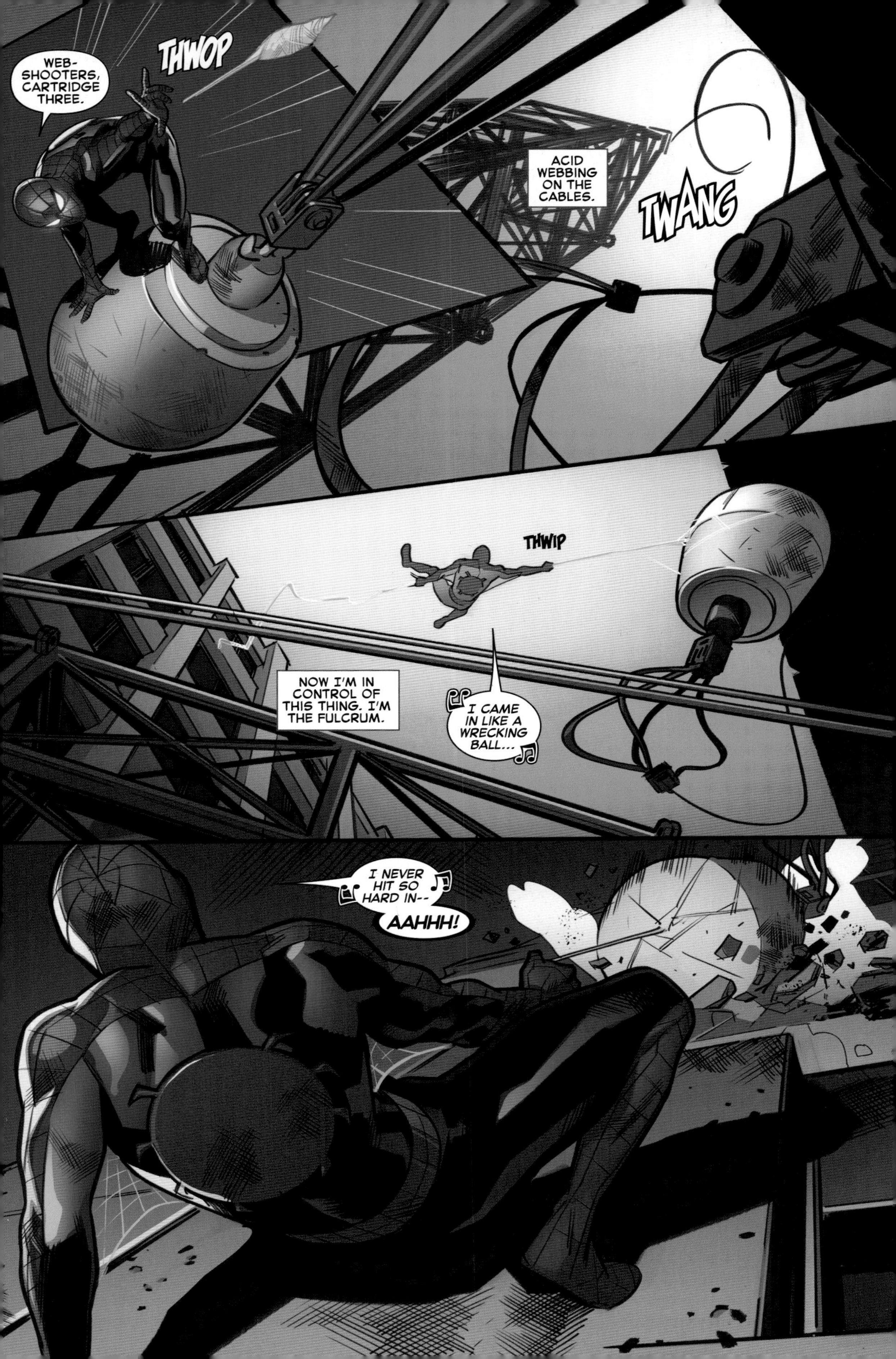
WEB-SHOOTERS, CARTRIDGE THREE.
THWOP
ACID WEBBING ON THE CABLES.
TWANG
THWIP
NOW I'M IN CONTROL OF THIS THING. I'M THE FULCRUM.
I CAME IN LIKE A WRECKING BALL...
I NEVER HIT SO HARD IN--
AAHHH!

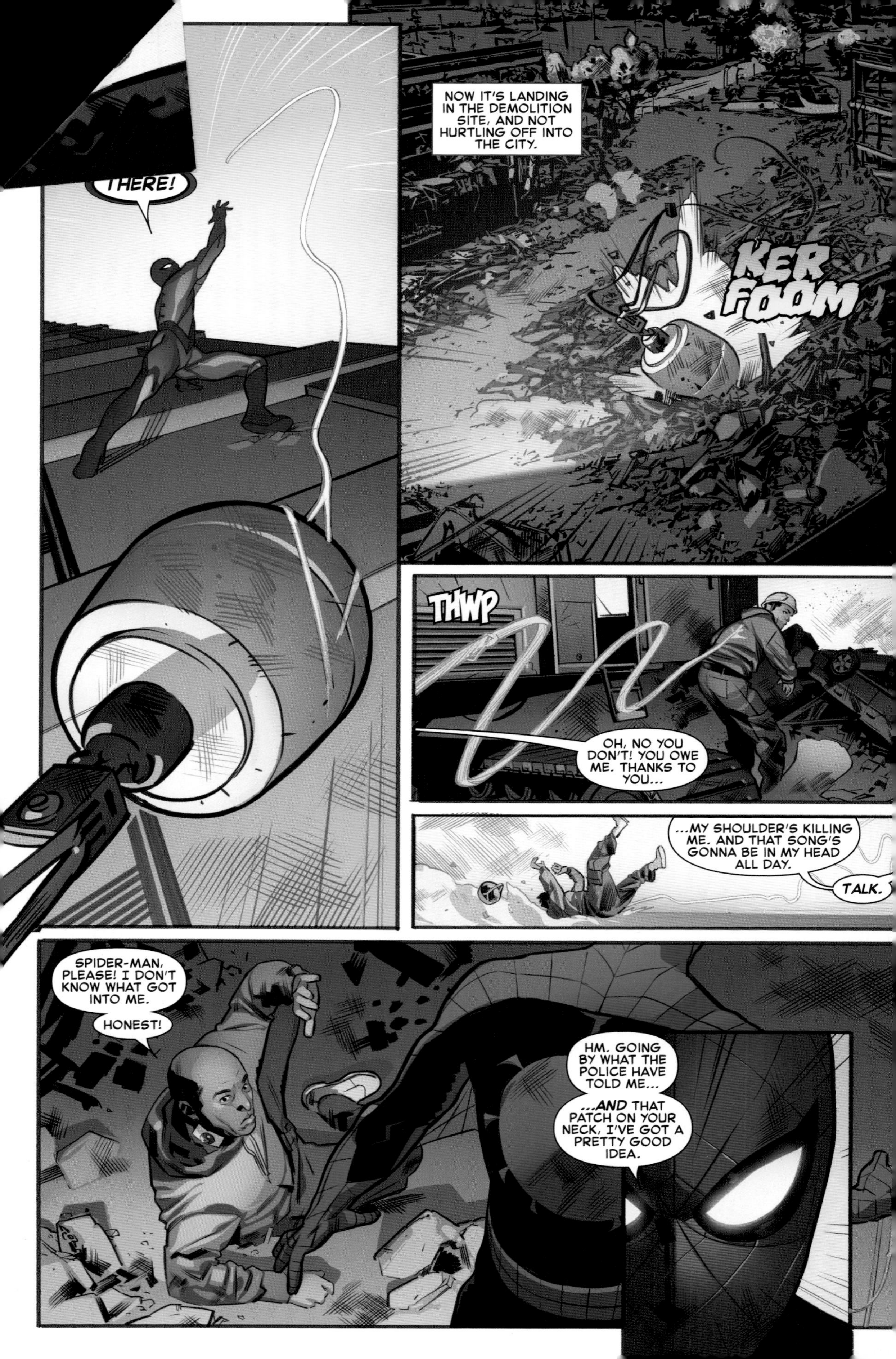
THERE!
NOW IT'S LANDING IN THE DEMOLITION SITE, AND NOT HURTLING OFF INTO THE CITY.
KER FOOM
THWP
OH, NO YOU DON'T! YOU OWE ME. THANKS TO YOU...
...MY SHOULDER'S KILLING ME. AND THAT SONG'S GONNA BE IN MY HEAD ALL DAY.
TALK.
SPIDER-MAN, PLEASE! I DON'T KNOW WHAT GOT INTO ME.
HONEST!
HM. GOING BY WHAT THE POLICE HAVE TOLD ME...
...AND THAT PATCH ON YOUR NECK, I'VE GOT A PRETTY GOOD IDEA.

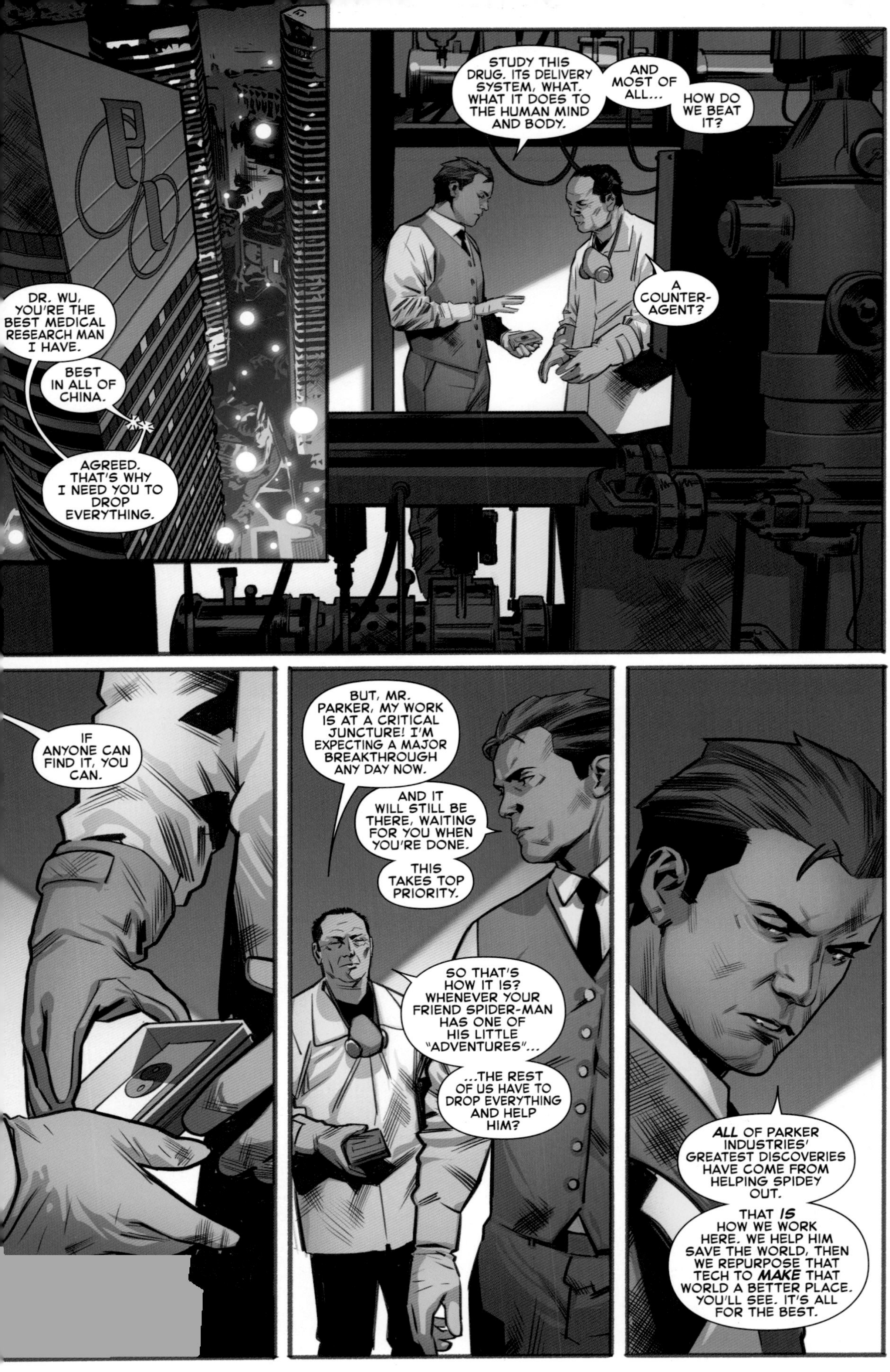
DR. WU, YOU'RE THE BEST MEDICAL RESEARCH MAN I HAVE.
BEST IN ALL OF CHINA.
AGREED. THAT'S WHY I NEED YOU TO DROP EVERYTHING.
STUDY THIS DRUG. ITS DELIVERY SYSTEM, WHAT. WHAT IT DOES TO THE HUMAN MIND AND BODY.
AND MOST OF ALL...
HOW DO WE BEAT IT?
A COUNTER-AGENT?
IF ANYONE CAN FIND IT, YOU CAN.
BUT, MR. PARKER, MY WORK IS AT A CRITICAL JUNCTURE! I'M EXPECTING A MAJOR BREAKTHROUGH ANY DAY NOW.
AND IT WILL STILL BE THERE, WAITING FOR YOU WHEN YOU'RE DONE.
THIS TAKES TOP PRIORITY.
SO THAT'S HOW IT IS? WHENEVER YOUR FRIEND SPIDER-MAN HAS ONE OF HIS LITTLE "ADVENTURES"...
...THE REST OF US HAVE TO DROP EVERYTHING AND HELP HIM?
ALL OF PARKER INDUSTRIES' GREATEST DISCOVERIES HAVE COME FROM HELPING SPIDEY OUT.
THAT IS HOW WE WORK HERE. WE HELP HIM SAVE THE WORLD, THEN WE REPURPOSE THAT TECH TO MAKE THAT WORLD A BETTER PLACE. YOU'LL SEE. IT'S ALL FOR THE BEST.

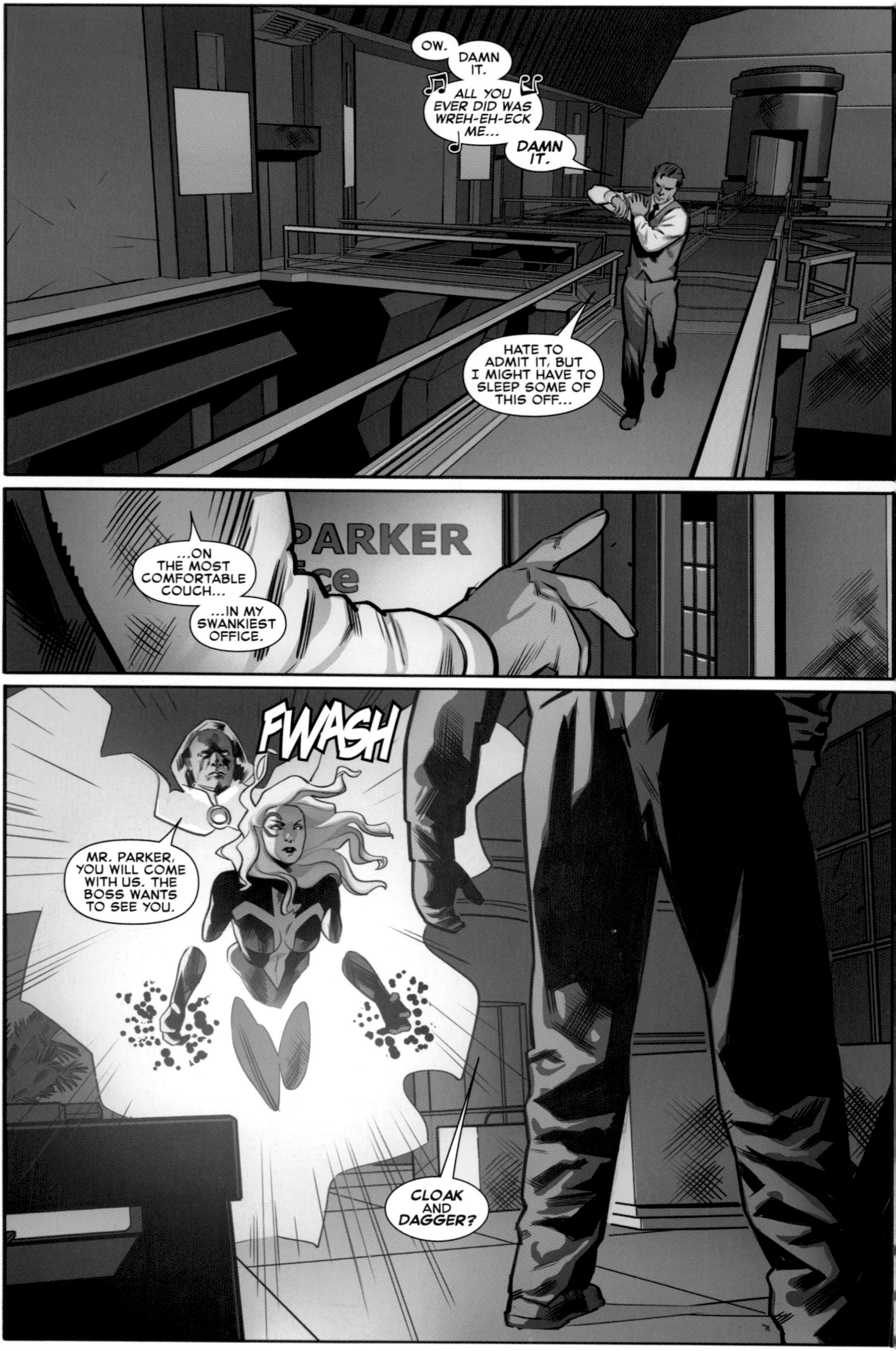

OW.
DAMN IT.
ALL YOU EVER DID WAS WREH-EH-ECK ME...
DAMN IT.
HATE TO ADMIT IT, BUT I MIGHT HAVE TO SLEEP SOME OF THIS OFF...
PARKER
...ON THE MOST COMFORTABLE COUCH...
...IN MY SWANKIEST OFFICE.
FWASH
MR. PARKER, YOU WILL COME WITH US. THE BOSS WANTS TO SEE YOU.
CLOAK AND DAGGER?

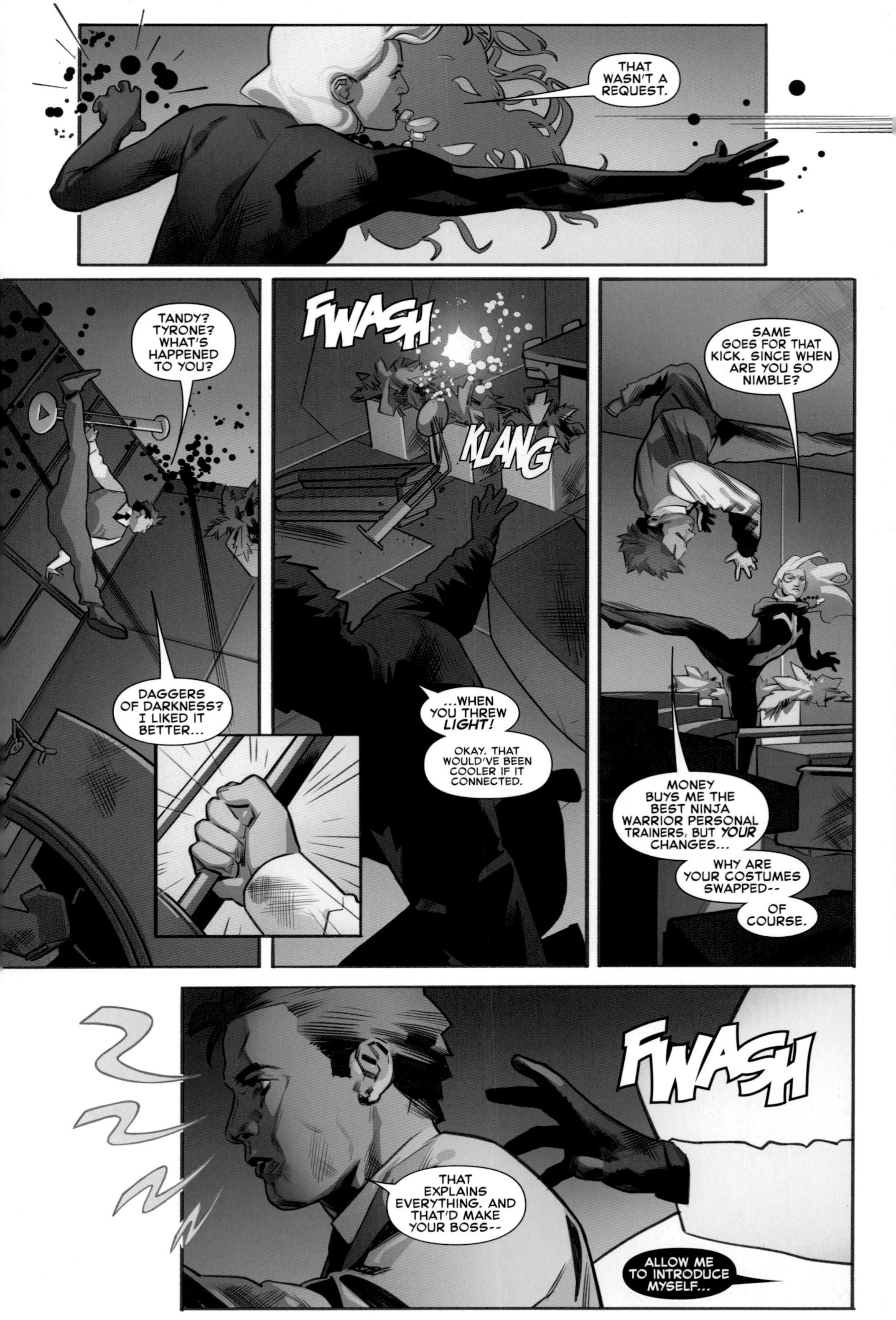
THAT WASN'T A REQUEST.
TANDY? TYRONE? WHAT'S HAPPENED TO YOU?
DAGGERS OF DARKNESS? I LIKED IT BETTER...
FWASH
KLANG
...WHEN YOU THREW LIGHT!
OKAY. THAT WOULD'VE BEEN COOLER IF IT CONNECTED.
SAME GOES FOR THAT KICK. SINCE WHEN ARE YOU SO NIMBLE?
MONEY BUYS ME THE BEST NINJA WARRIOR PERSONAL TRAINERS, BUT YOUR CHANGES...
WHY ARE YOUR COSTUMES SWAPPED--
OF COURSE.
FWASH
THAT EXPLAINS EVERYTHING. AND THAT'D MAKE YOUR BOSS--
ALLOW ME TO INTRODUCE MYSELF...

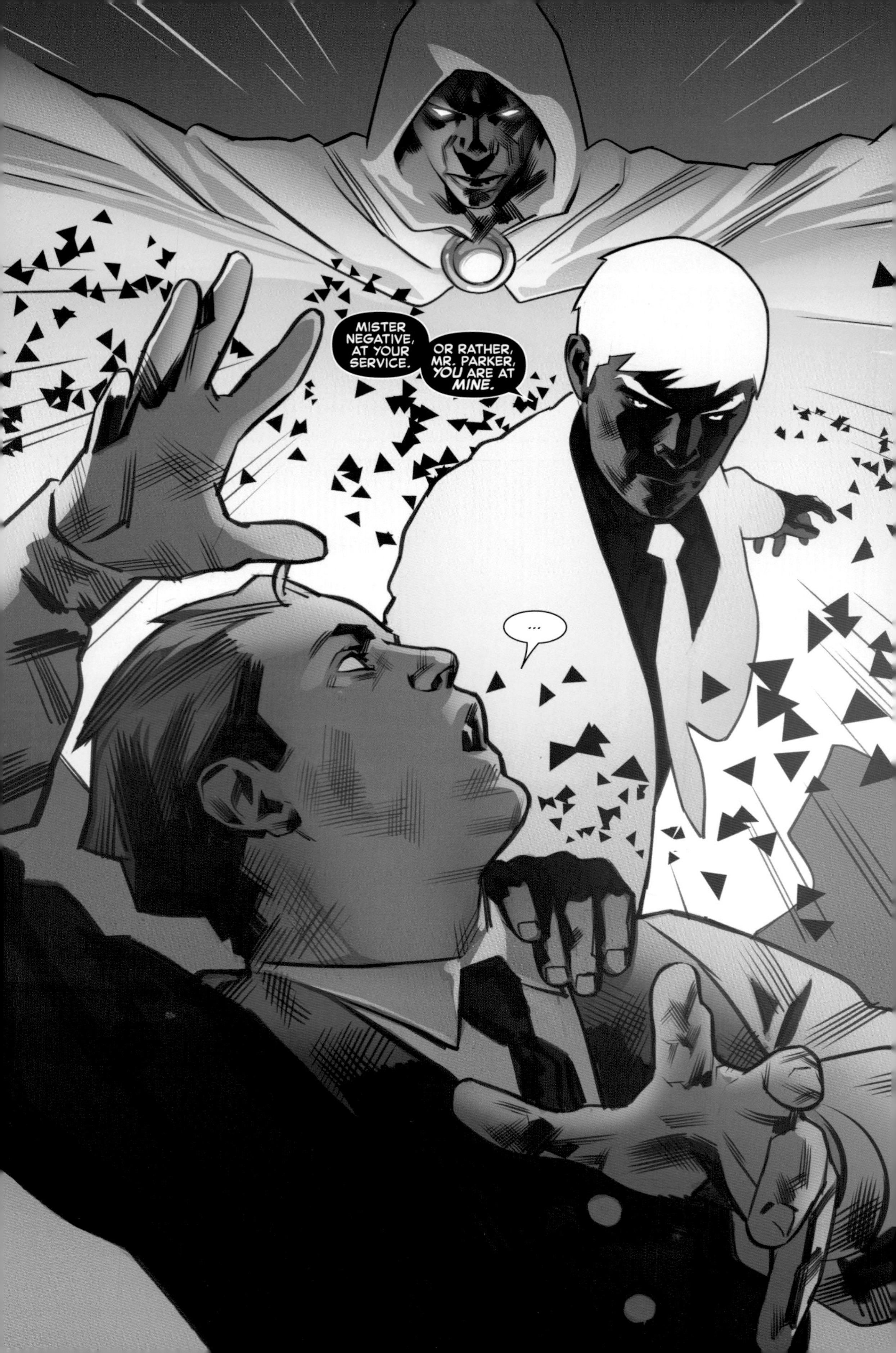
MISTER NEGATIVE, AT YOUR SERVICE.
OR RATHER, MR. PARKER, YOU ARE AT MINE.
...

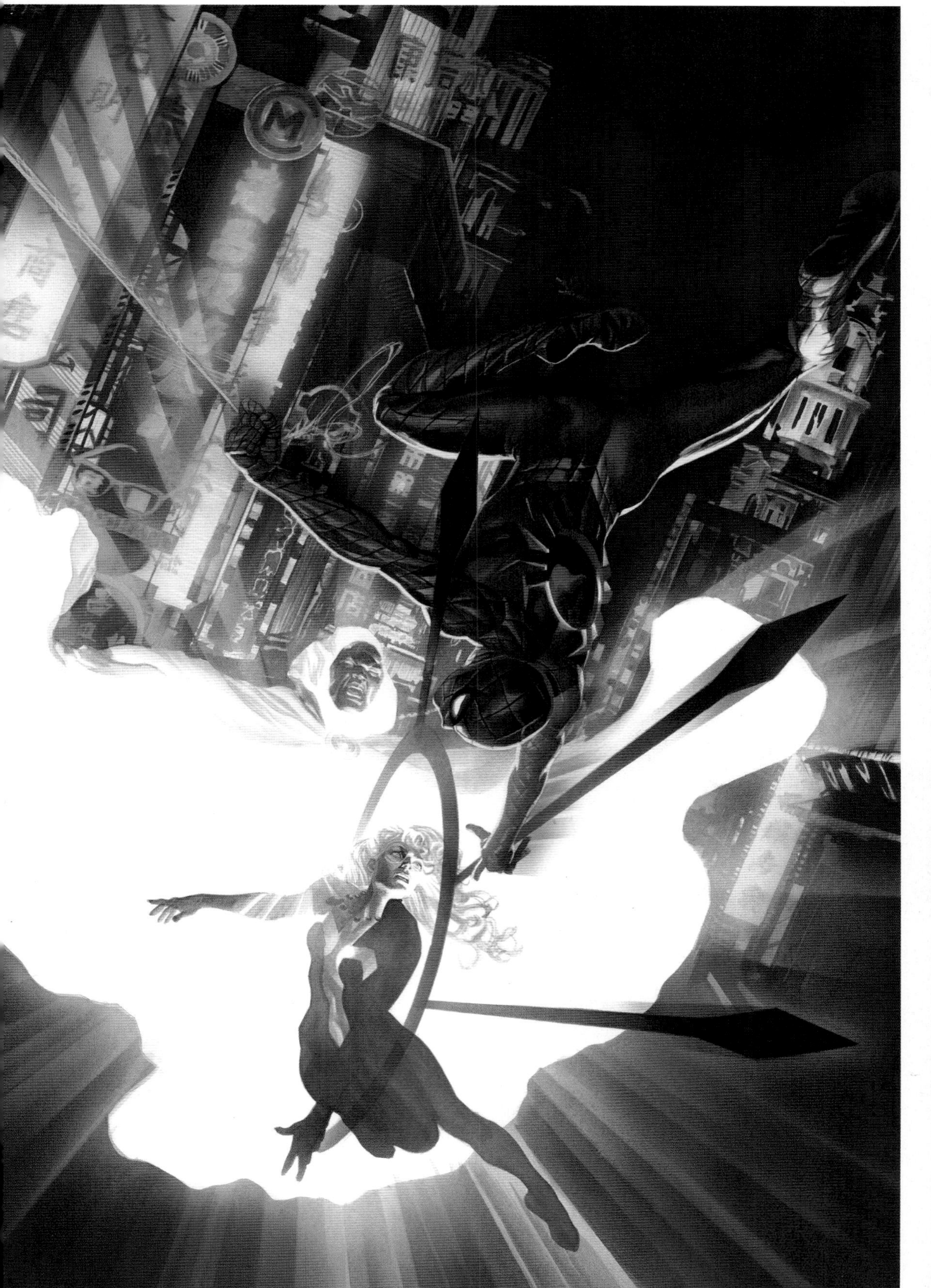

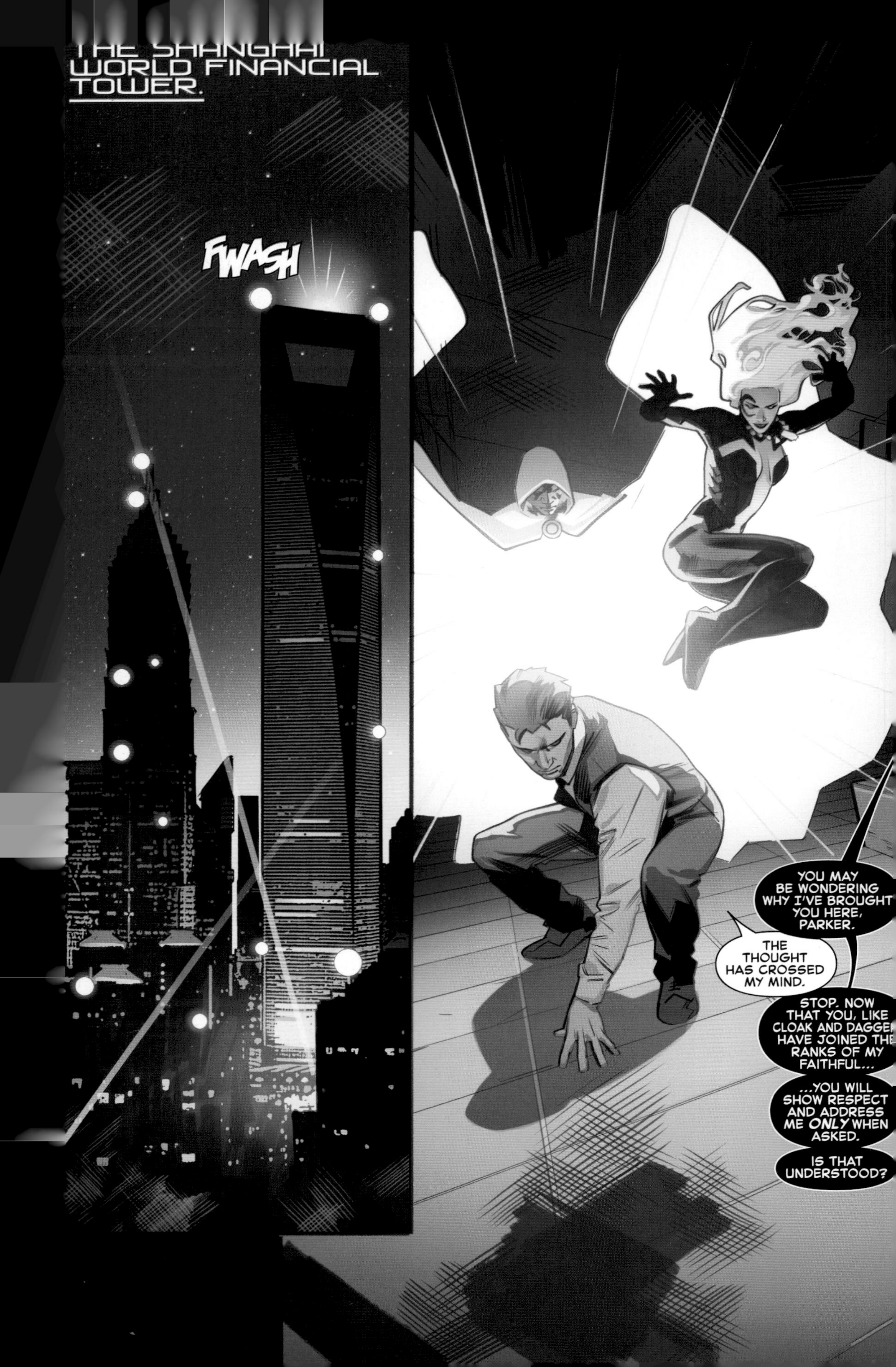
THE SHANGHAI WORLD FINANCIAL TOWER.
FWASH
YOU MAY BE WONDERING WHY I'VE BROUGHT YOU HERE, PARKER.
THE THOUGHT HAS CROSSED MY MIND.
STOP. NOW THAT YOU, LIKE CLOAK AND DAGGER, HAVE JOINED THE RANKS OF MY FAITHFUL...
...YOU WILL SHOW RESPECT AND ADDRESS ME ONLY WHEN ASKED.
IS THAT UNDERSTOOD?

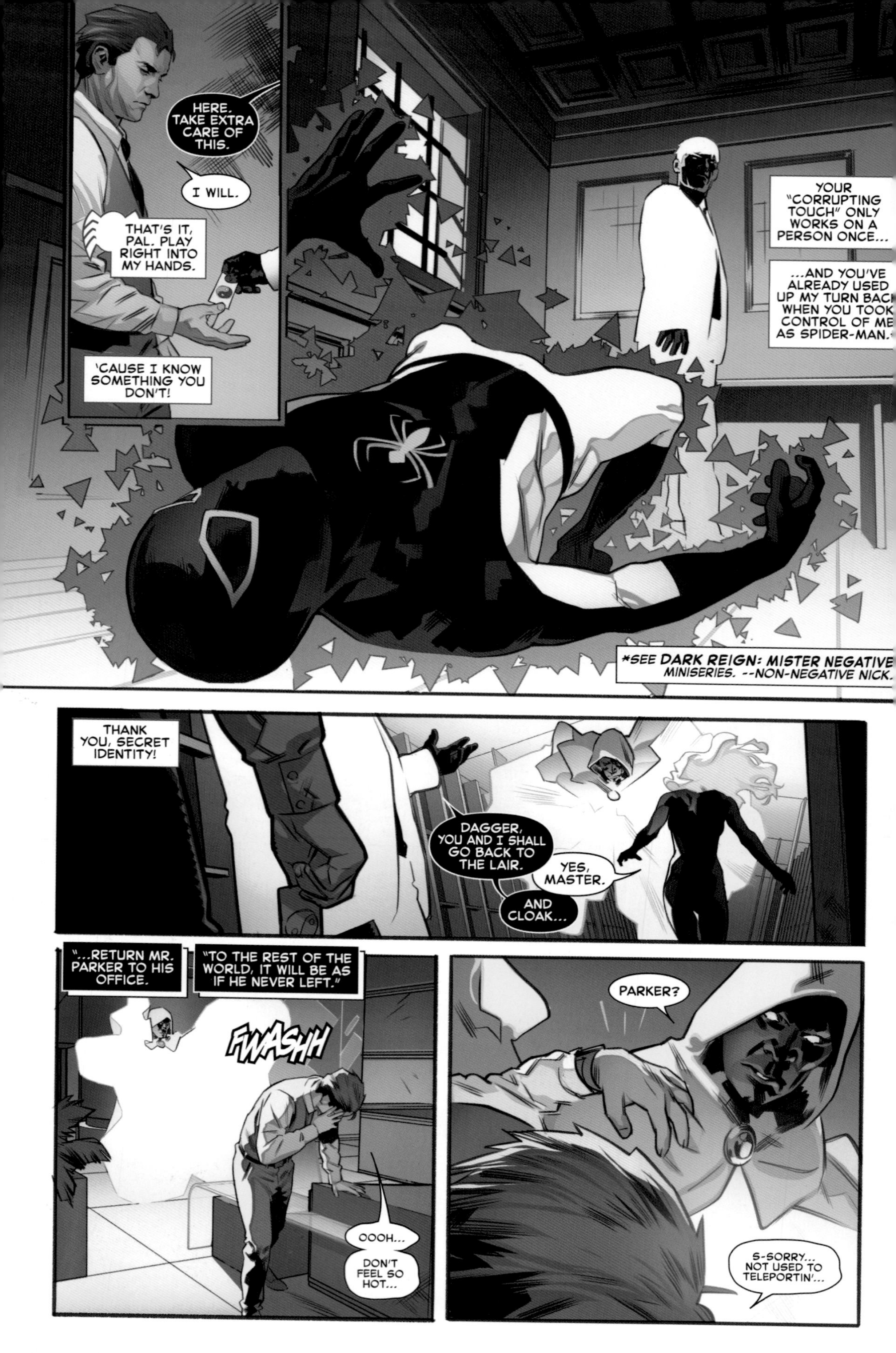
HERE. TAKE EXTRA CARE OF THIS.
I WILL.
THAT'S IT, PAL. PLAY RIGHT INTO MY HANDS.
'CAUSE I KNOW SOMETHING YOU DON'T!
YOUR "CORRUPTING TOUCH" ONLY WORKS ON A PERSON ONCE...
...AND YOU'VE ALREADY USED UP MY TURN BACK WHEN YOU TOOK CONTROL OF ME AS SPIDER-MAN.*
*SEE DARK REIGN: MISTER NEGATIVE MINISERIES. --NON-NEGATIVE NICK.
THANK YOU, SECRET IDENTITY!
DAGGER, YOU AND I SHALL GO BACK TO THE LAIR.
YES, MASTER.
AND CLOAK...
"...RETURN MR. PARKER TO HIS OFFICE.
"TO THE REST OF THE WORLD, IT WILL BE AS IF HE NEVER LEFT."
FWASHH
OOOH...
DON'T FEEL SO HOT...
PARKER?
S-SORRY... NOT USED TO TELEPORTIN'...

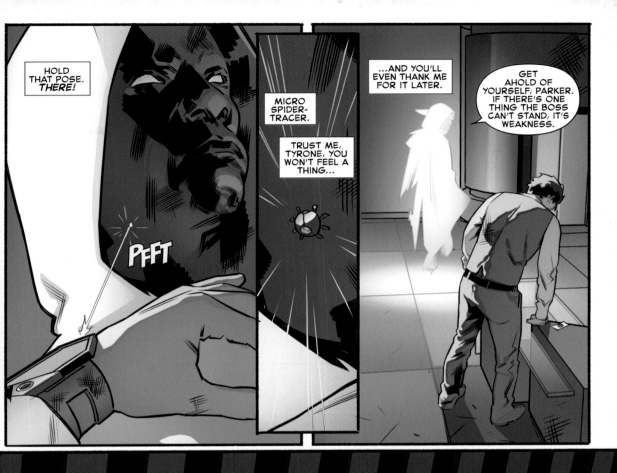

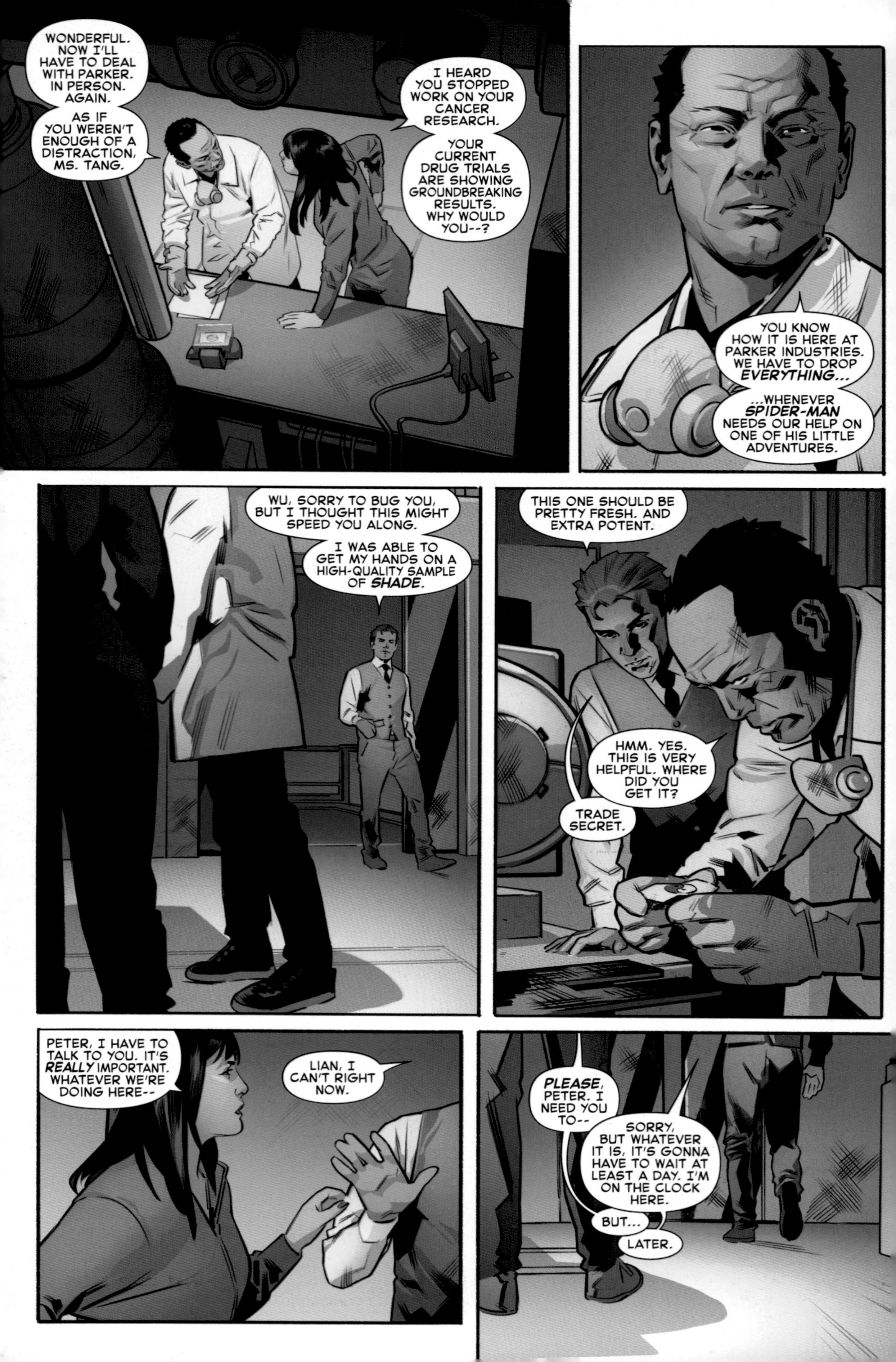
WONDERFUL. NOW I'LL HAVE TO DEAL WITH PARKER. IN PERSON. AGAIN.
AS IF YOU WEREN'T ENOUGH OF A DISTRACTION, MS. TANG.
I HEARD YOU STOPPED WORK ON YOUR CANCER RESEARCH.
YOUR CURRENT DRUG TRIALS ARE SHOWING GROUNDBREAKING RESULTS. WHY WOULD YOU--?
YOU KNOW HOW IT IS HERE AT PARKER INDUSTRIES. WE HAVE TO DROP EVERYTHING...
...WHENEVER SPIDER-MAN NEEDS OUR HELP ON ONE OF HIS LITTLE ADVENTURES.
WU, SORRY TO BUG YOU, BUT I THOUGHT THIS MIGHT SPEED YOU ALONG.
I WAS ABLE TO GET MY HANDS ON A HIGH-QUALITY SAMPLE OF SHADE.
THIS ONE SHOULD BE PRETTY FRESH. AND EXTRA POTENT.
HMM. YES. THIS IS VERY HELPFUL. WHERE DID YOU GET IT?
TRADE SECRET.
PETER, I HAVE TO TALK TO YOU. IT'S REALLY IMPORTANT. WHATEVER WE'RE DOING HERE--
LIAN, I CAN'T RIGHT NOW.
PLEASE, PETER. I NEED YOU TO--
SORRY, BUT WHATEVER IT IS, IT'S GONNA HAVE TO WAIT AT LEAST A DAY. I'M ON THE CLOCK HERE.
BUT...
LATER.

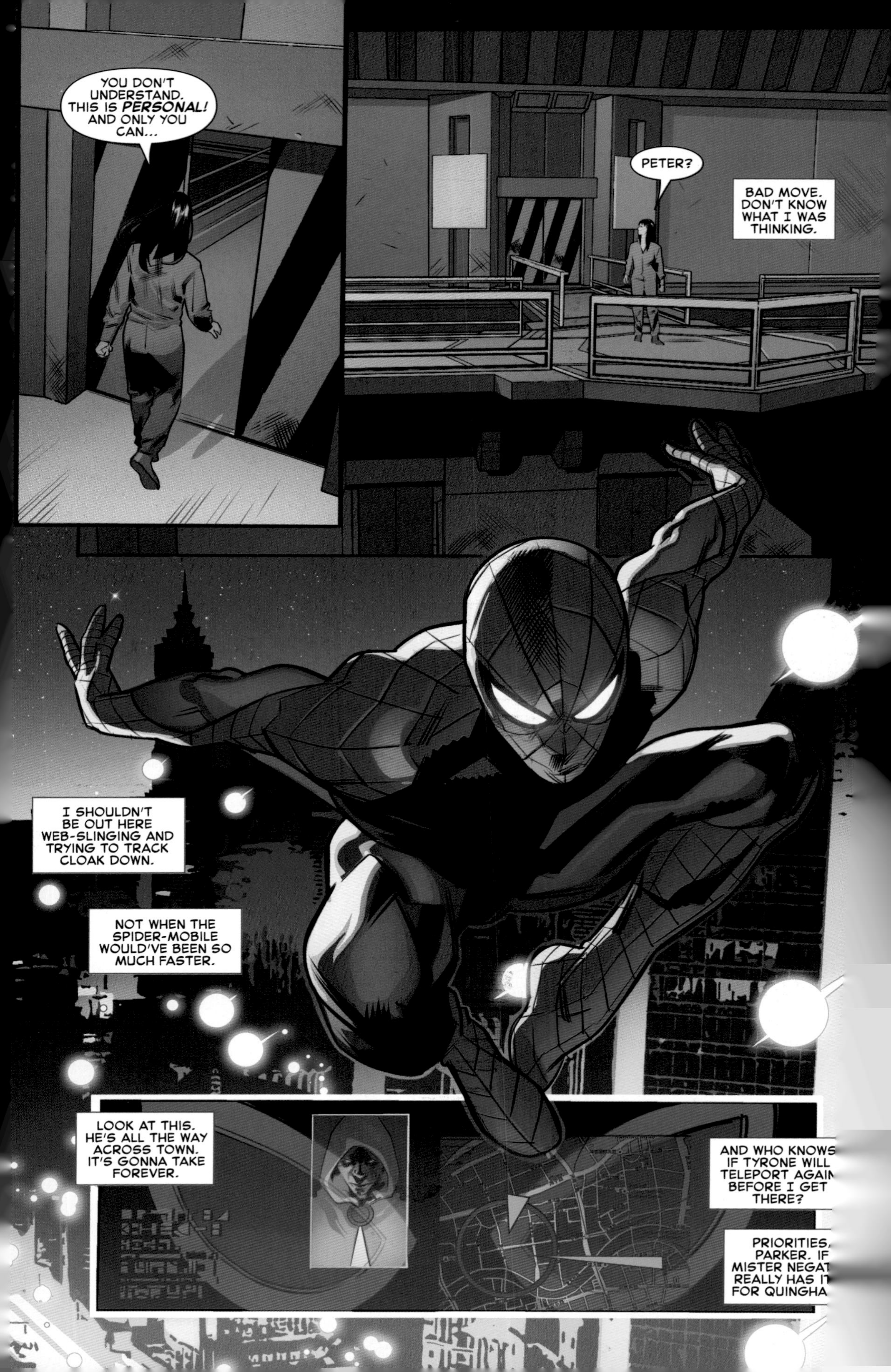
YOU DON'T UNDERSTAND. THIS IS PERSONAL! AND ONLY YOU CAN...
PETER?
BAD MOVE. DON'T KNOW WHAT I WAS THINKING.
I SHOULDN'T BE OUT HERE WEB-SLINGING AND TRYING TO TRACK CLOAK DOWN.
NOT WHEN THE SPIDER-MOBILE WOULD'VE BEEN SO MUCH FASTER.
LOOK AT THIS. HE'S ALL THE WAY ACROSS TOWN. IT'S GONNA TAKE FOREVER.
AND WHO KNOWS IF TYRONE WILL TELEPORT AGAIN BEFORE I GET THERE?
PRIORITIES, PARKER. IF MISTER NEGAT REALLY HAS IT FOR QUINGHA

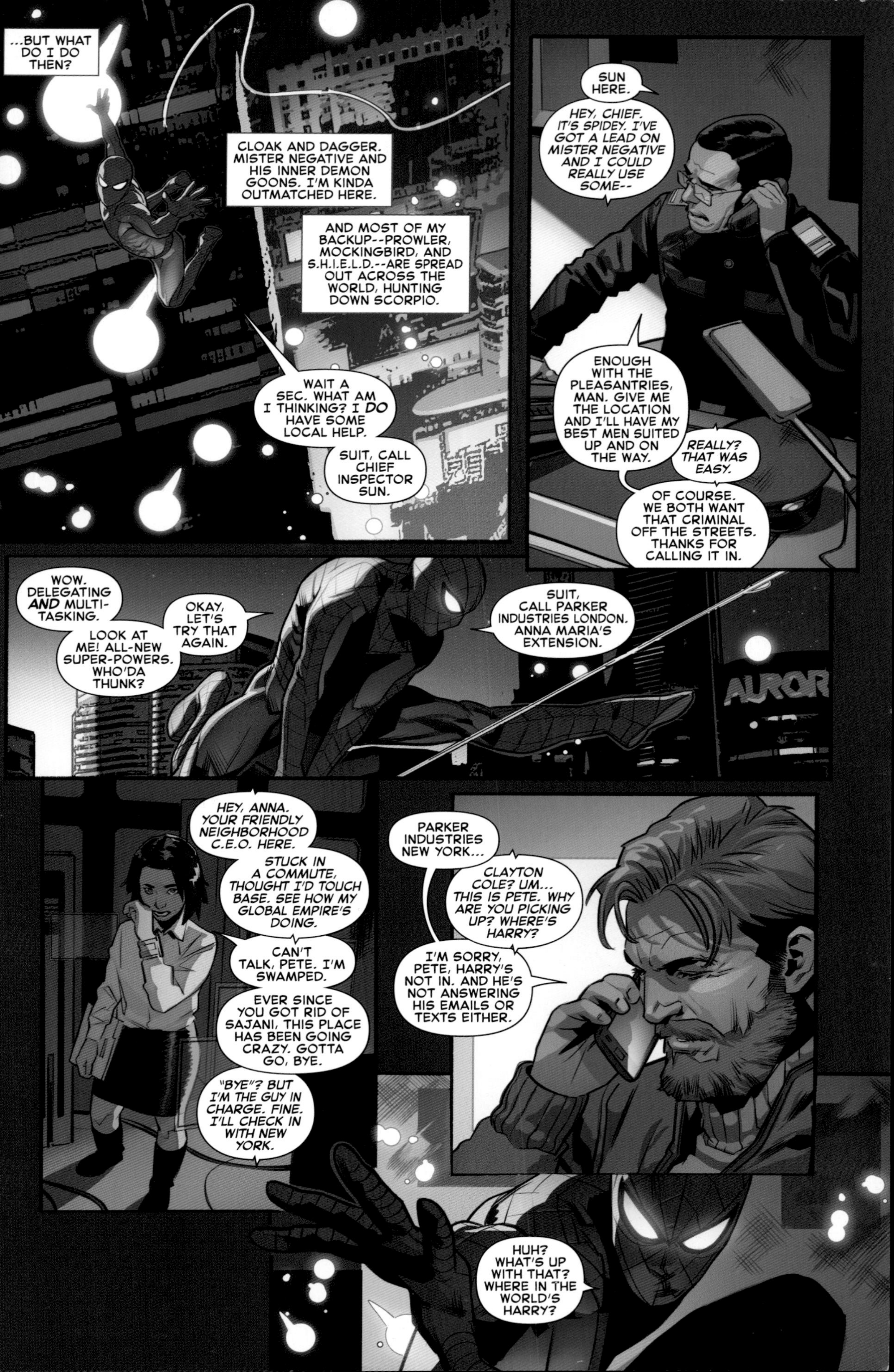
...BUT WHAT DO I DO THEN?
CLOAK AND DAGGER. MISTER NEGATIVE AND HIS INNER DEMON GOONS. I'M KINDA OUTMATCHED HERE.
AND MOST OF MY BACKUP--PROWLER, MOCKINGBIRD, AND S.H.I.E.L.D.--ARE SPREAD OUT ACROSS THE WORLD, HUNTING DOWN SCORPIO.
WAIT A SEC. WHAT AM I THINKING? I *DO* HAVE SOME LOCAL HELP.
SUIT, CALL CHIEF INSPECTOR SUN.
SUN HERE.
HEY, CHIEF. IT'S SPIDEY. I'VE GOT A LEAD ON MISTER NEGATIVE AND I COULD REALLY USE SOME--
ENOUGH WITH THE PLEASANTRIES, MAN. GIVE ME THE LOCATION AND I'LL HAVE MY BEST MEN SUITED UP AND ON THE WAY.
REALLY? THAT WAS EASY.
OF COURSE. WE BOTH WANT THAT CRIMINAL OFF THE STREETS. THANKS FOR CALLING IT IN.
WOW. DELEGATING ***AND*** MULTI-TASKING.
LOOK AT ME! ALL-NEW SUPER-POWERS. WHO'DA THUNK?
OKAY, LET'S TRY THAT AGAIN.
SUIT, CALL PARKER INDUSTRIES LONDON. ANNA MARIA'S EXTENSION.
AUROR
HEY, ANNA. YOUR FRIENDLY NEIGHBORHOOD C.E.O. HERE.
STUCK IN A COMMUTE, THOUGHT I'D TOUCH BASE. SEE HOW MY GLOBAL EMPIRE'S DOING.
CAN'T TALK, PETE. I'M SWAMPED.
EVER SINCE YOU GOT RID OF SAJANI, THIS PLACE HAS BEEN GOING CRAZY. GOTTA GO, BYE.
"BYE"? BUT I'M THE GUY IN CHARGE. FINE. I'LL CHECK IN WITH NEW YORK.
PARKER INDUSTRIES NEW YORK...
CLAYTON COLE? UM... THIS IS PETE. WHY ARE YOU PICKING UP? WHERE'S HARRY?
I'M SORRY, PETE, HARRY'S NOT IN. AND HE'S NOT ANSWERING HIS EMAILS OR TEXTS EITHER.
HUH? WHAT'S UP WITH THAT? WHERE IN THE WORLD'S HARRY?

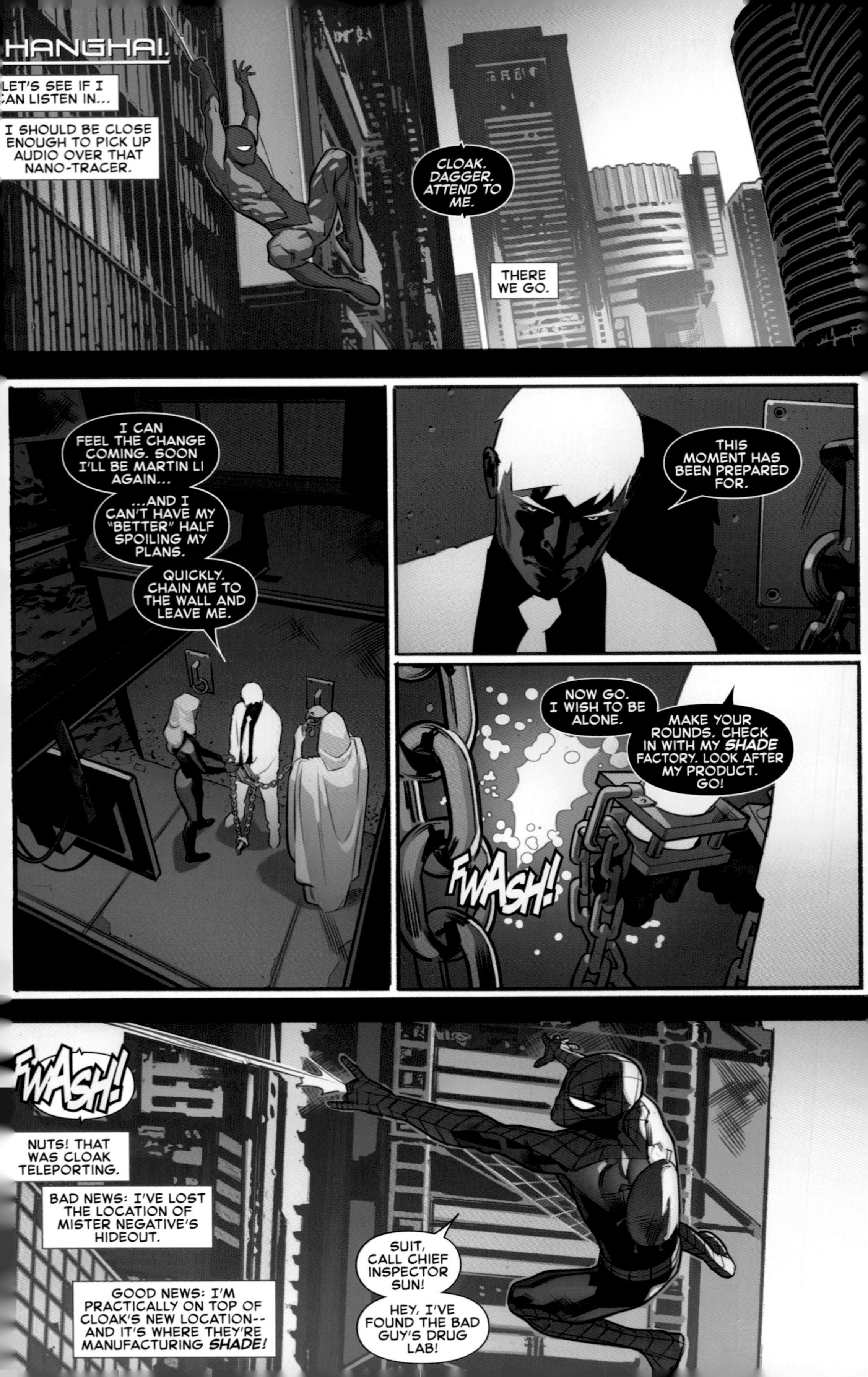

SHANGHAI.
LET'S SEE IF I CAN LISTEN IN...
I SHOULD BE CLOSE ENOUGH TO PICK UP AUDIO OVER THAT NANO-TRACER.
CLOAK. DAGGER. ATTEND TO ME.
THERE WE GO.
I CAN FEEL THE CHANGE COMING. SOON I'LL BE MARTIN LI AGAIN...
...AND I CAN'T HAVE MY "BETTER" HALF SPOILING MY PLANS.
QUICKLY. CHAIN ME TO THE WALL AND LEAVE ME.
THIS MOMENT HAS BEEN PREPARED FOR.
NOW GO. I WISH TO BE ALONE.
MAKE YOUR ROUNDS. CHECK IN WITH MY SHADE FACTORY. LOOK AFTER MY PRODUCT. GO!
FWASH!
FWASH!
NUTS! THAT WAS CLOAK TELEPORTING.
BAD NEWS: I'VE LOST THE LOCATION OF MISTER NEGATIVE'S HIDEOUT.
GOOD NEWS: I'M PRACTICALLY ON TOP OF CLOAK'S NEW LOCATION--AND IT'S WHERE THEY'RE MANUFACTURING SHADE!
SUIT, CALL CHIEF INSPECTOR SUN!
HEY, I'VE FOUND THE BAD GUY'S DRUG LAB!

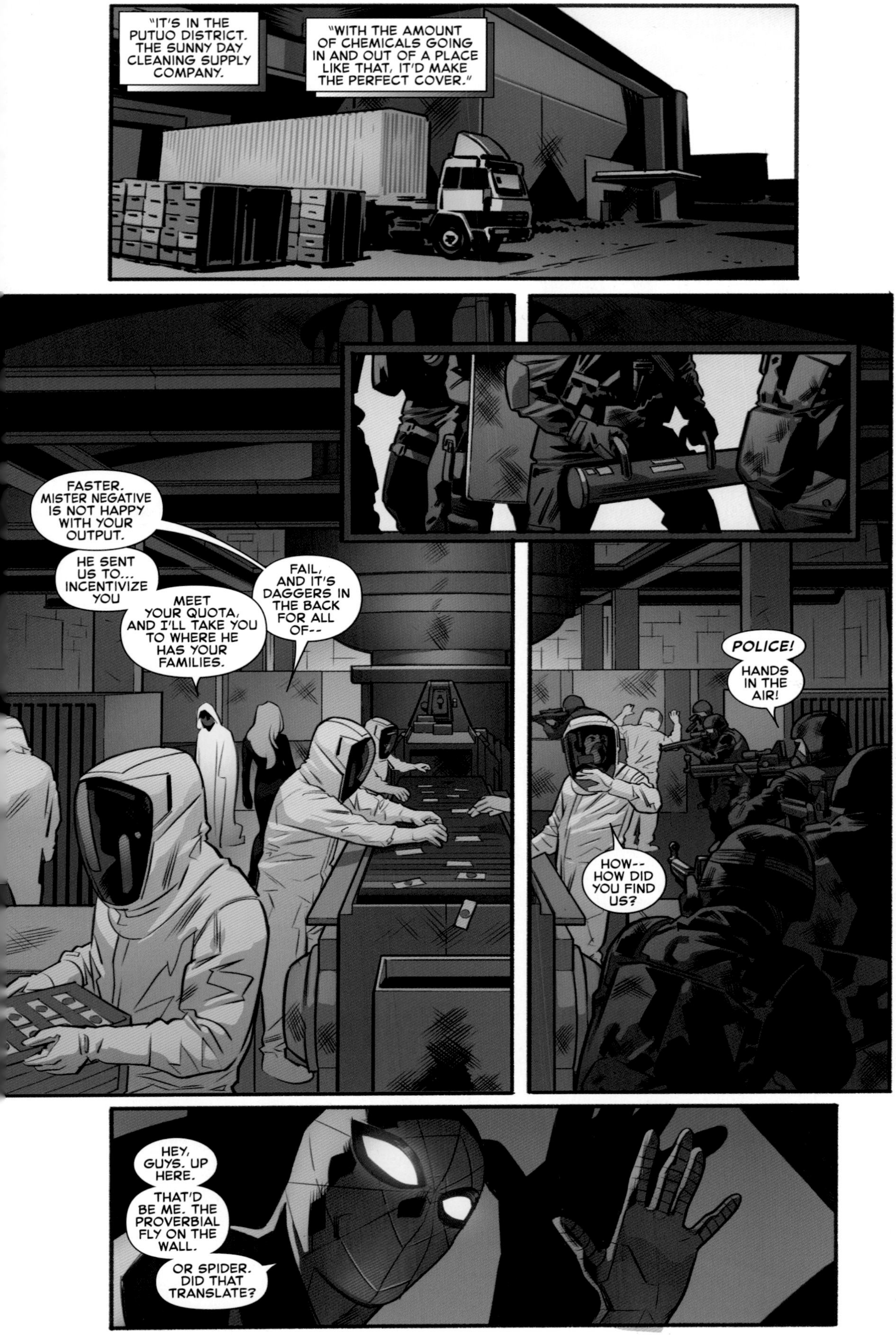
"IT'S IN THE PUTUO DISTRICT. THE SUNNY DAY CLEANING SUPPLY COMPANY.
"WITH THE AMOUNT OF CHEMICALS GOING IN AND OUT OF A PLACE LIKE THAT, IT'D MAKE THE PERFECT COVER."
FASTER. MISTER NEGATIVE IS NOT HAPPY WITH YOUR OUTPUT.
HE SENT US TO... INCENTIVIZE YOU
MEET YOUR QUOTA, AND I'LL TAKE YOU TO WHERE HE HAS YOUR FAMILIES.
FAIL, AND IT'S DAGGERS IN THE BACK FOR ALL OF--
POLICE!
HANDS IN THE AIR!
HOW-- HOW DID YOU FIND US?
HEY, GUYS. UP HERE.
THAT'D BE ME. THE PROVERBIAL FLY ON THE WALL.
OR SPIDER. DID THAT TRANSLATE?

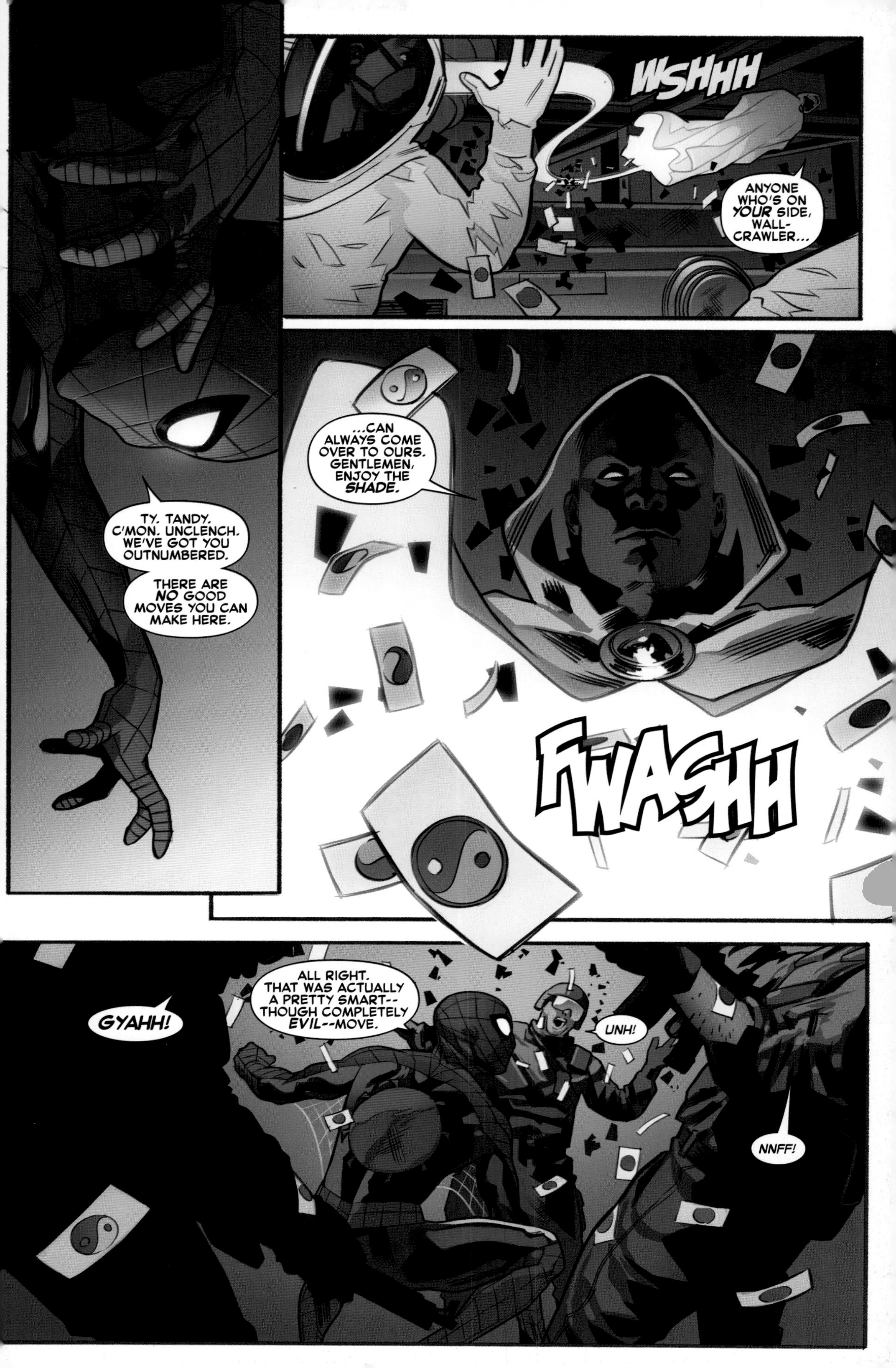
WSHHH
ANYONE WHO'S ON YOUR SIDE, WALL-CRAWLER...
TY. TANDY. C'MON. UNCLENCH. WE'VE GOT YOU OUTNUMBERED.
THERE ARE NO GOOD MOVES YOU CAN MAKE HERE.
...CAN ALWAYS COME OVER TO OURS. GENTLEMEN, ENJOY THE SHADE.
FWASHH
GYAHH!
ALL RIGHT. THAT WAS ACTUALLY A PRETTY SMART--THOUGH COMPLETELY EVIL--MOVE.
UNH!
NNFF!

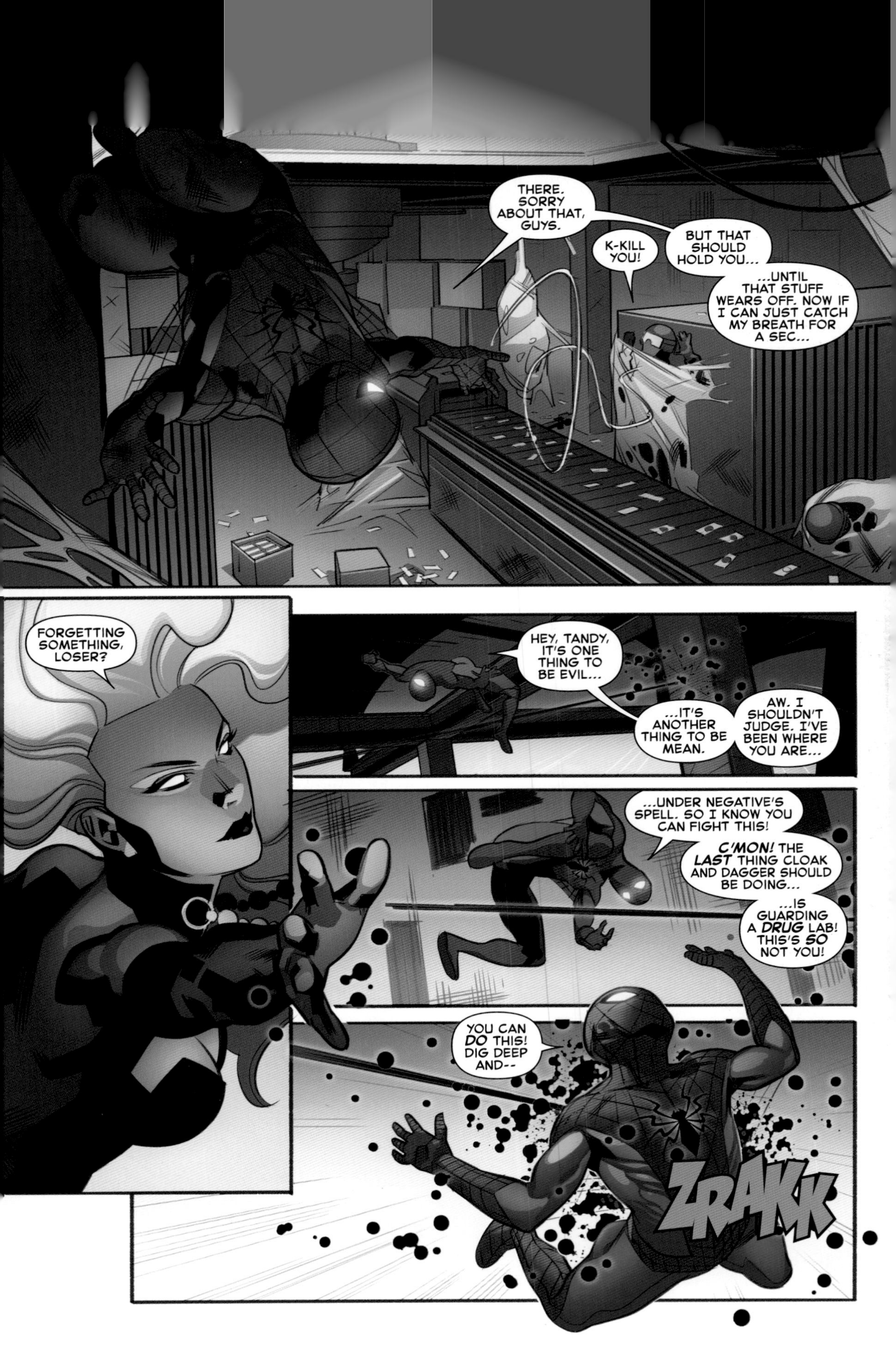
THERE. SORRY ABOUT THAT, GUYS.
K-KILL YOU!
BUT THAT SHOULD HOLD YOU...
...UNTIL THAT STUFF WEARS OFF. NOW IF I CAN JUST CATCH MY BREATH FOR A SEC...
FORGETTING SOMETHING, LOSER?
HEY, TANDY, IT'S ONE THING TO BE EVIL...
...IT'S ANOTHER THING TO BE MEAN.
AW. I SHOULDN'T JUDGE. I'VE BEEN WHERE YOU ARE...
...UNDER NEGATIVE'S SPELL. SO I KNOW YOU CAN FIGHT THIS!
C'MON! THE LAST THING CLOAK AND DAGGER SHOULD BE DOING...
...IS GUARDING A DRUG LAB! THIS'S SO NOT YOU!
YOU CAN DO THIS! DIG DEEP AND--
ZRAKK

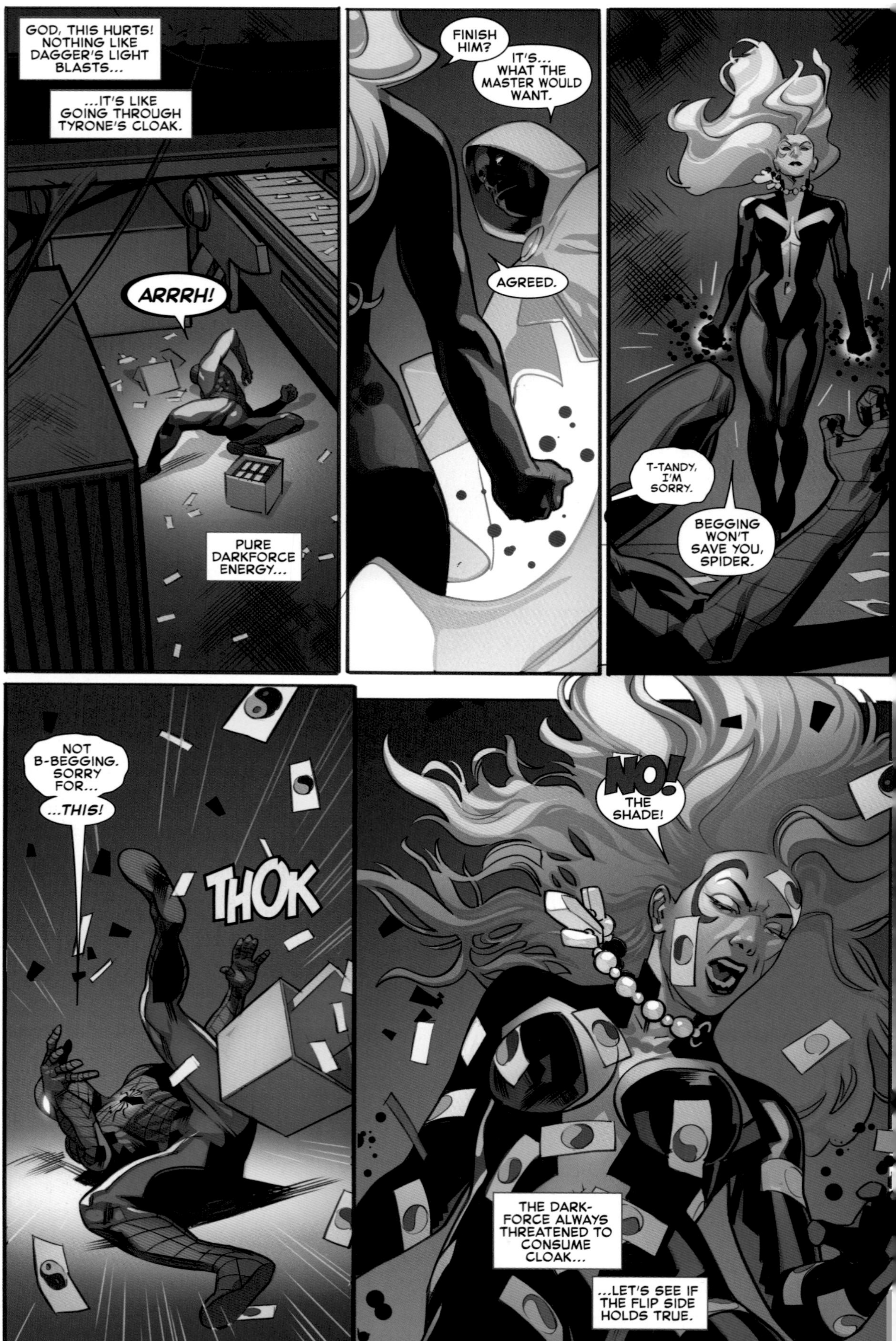
GOD, THIS HURTS! NOTHING LIKE DAGGER'S LIGHT BLASTS...
...IT'S LIKE GOING THROUGH TYRONE'S CLOAK.
ARRRH!
PURE DARKFORCE ENERGY...
FINISH HIM?
IT'S... WHAT THE MASTER WOULD WANT.
AGREED.
T-TANDY, I'M SORRY.
BEGGING WON'T SAVE YOU, SPIDER.
NOT B-BEGGING. SORRY FOR...
...THIS!
THOK
NO! THE SHADE!
THE DARK-FORCE ALWAYS THREATENED TO CONSUME CLOAK...
...LET'S SEE IF THE FLIP SIDE HOLDS TRUE.

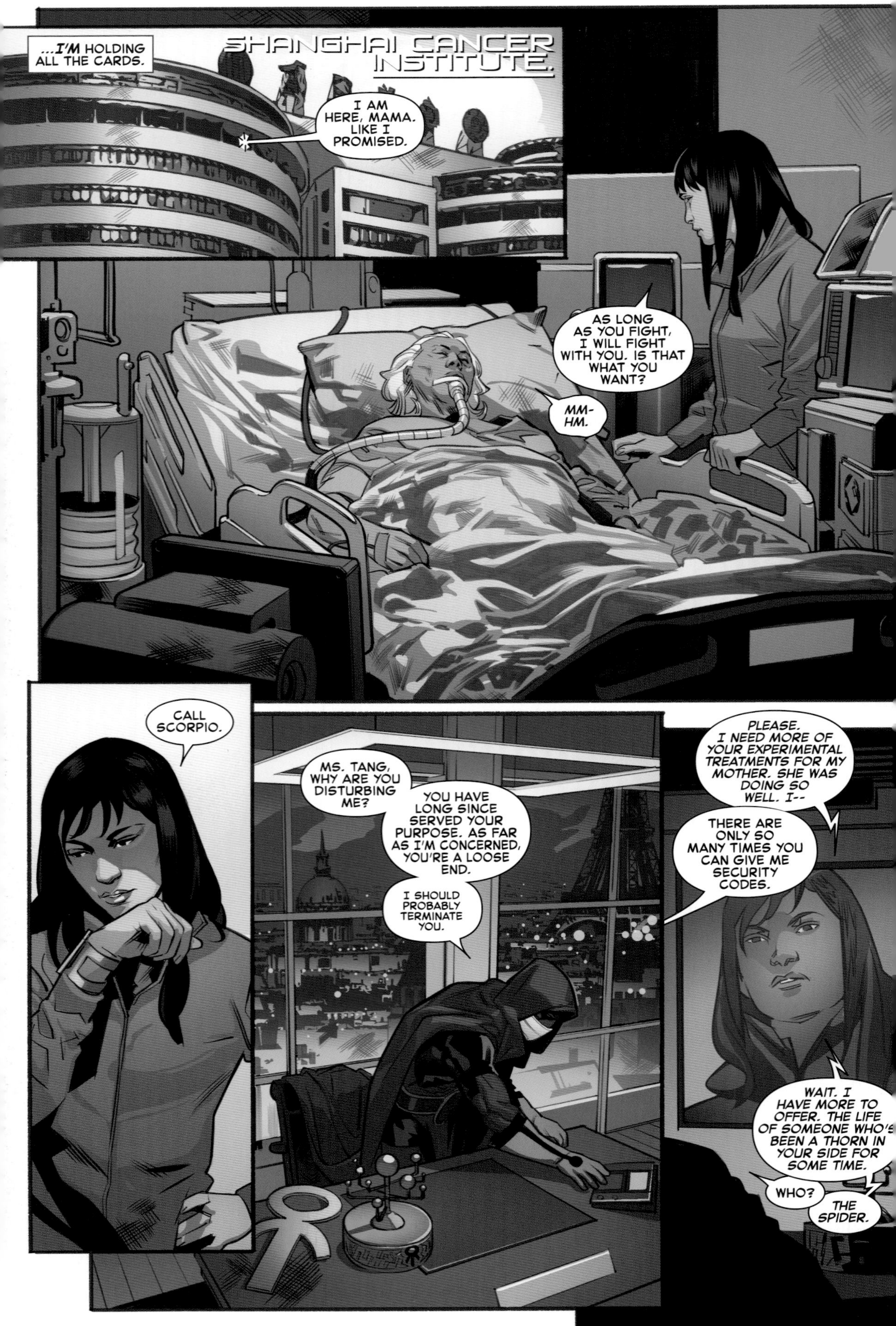
...I'M HOLDING ALL THE CARDS.
SHANGHAI CANCER INSTITUTE.
I AM HERE, MAMA. LIKE I PROMISED.
AS LONG AS YOU FIGHT, I WILL FIGHT WITH YOU. IS THAT WHAT YOU WANT?
MM-HM.
CALL SCORPIO.
MS. TANG, WHY ARE YOU DISTURBING ME?
YOU HAVE LONG SINCE SERVED YOUR PURPOSE. AS FAR AS I'M CONCERNED, YOU'RE A LOOSE END.
I SHOULD PROBABLY TERMINATE YOU.
PLEASE. I NEED MORE OF YOUR EXPERIMENTAL TREATMENTS FOR MY MOTHER. SHE WAS DOING SO WELL. I--
THERE ARE ONLY SO MANY TIMES YOU CAN GIVE ME SECURITY CODES.
WAIT. I HAVE MORE TO OFFER. THE LIFE OF SOMEONE WHO'S BEEN A THORN IN YOUR SIDE FOR SOME TIME.
WHO?
THE SPIDER.

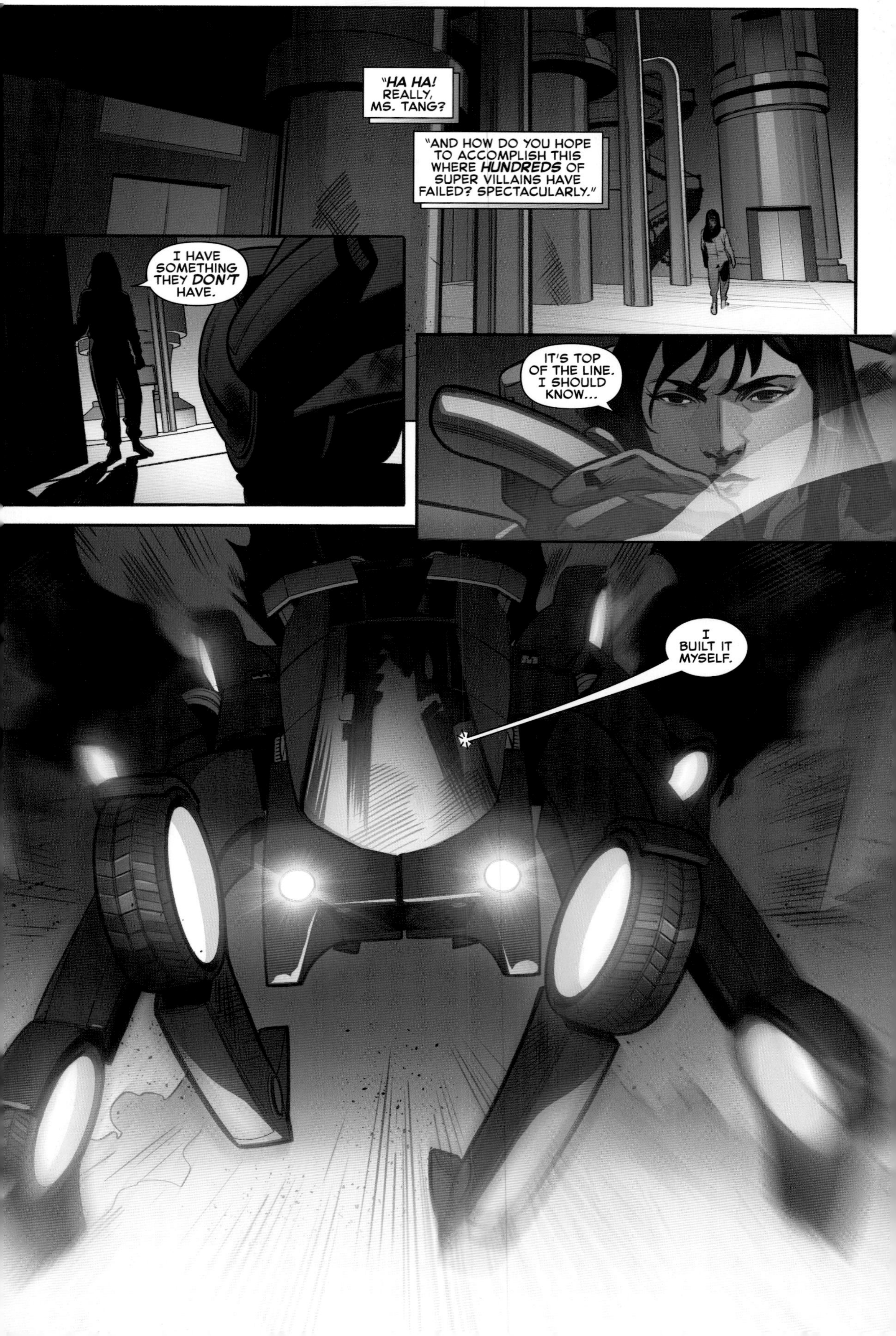
"HA HA! REALLY, MS. TANG?
"AND HOW DO YOU HOPE TO ACCOMPLISH THIS WHERE HUNDREDS OF SUPER VILLAINS HAVE FAILED? SPECTACULARLY."
I HAVE SOMETHING THEY DON'T HAVE.
IT'S TOP OF THE LINE. I SHOULD KNOW...
I BUILT IT MYSELF.

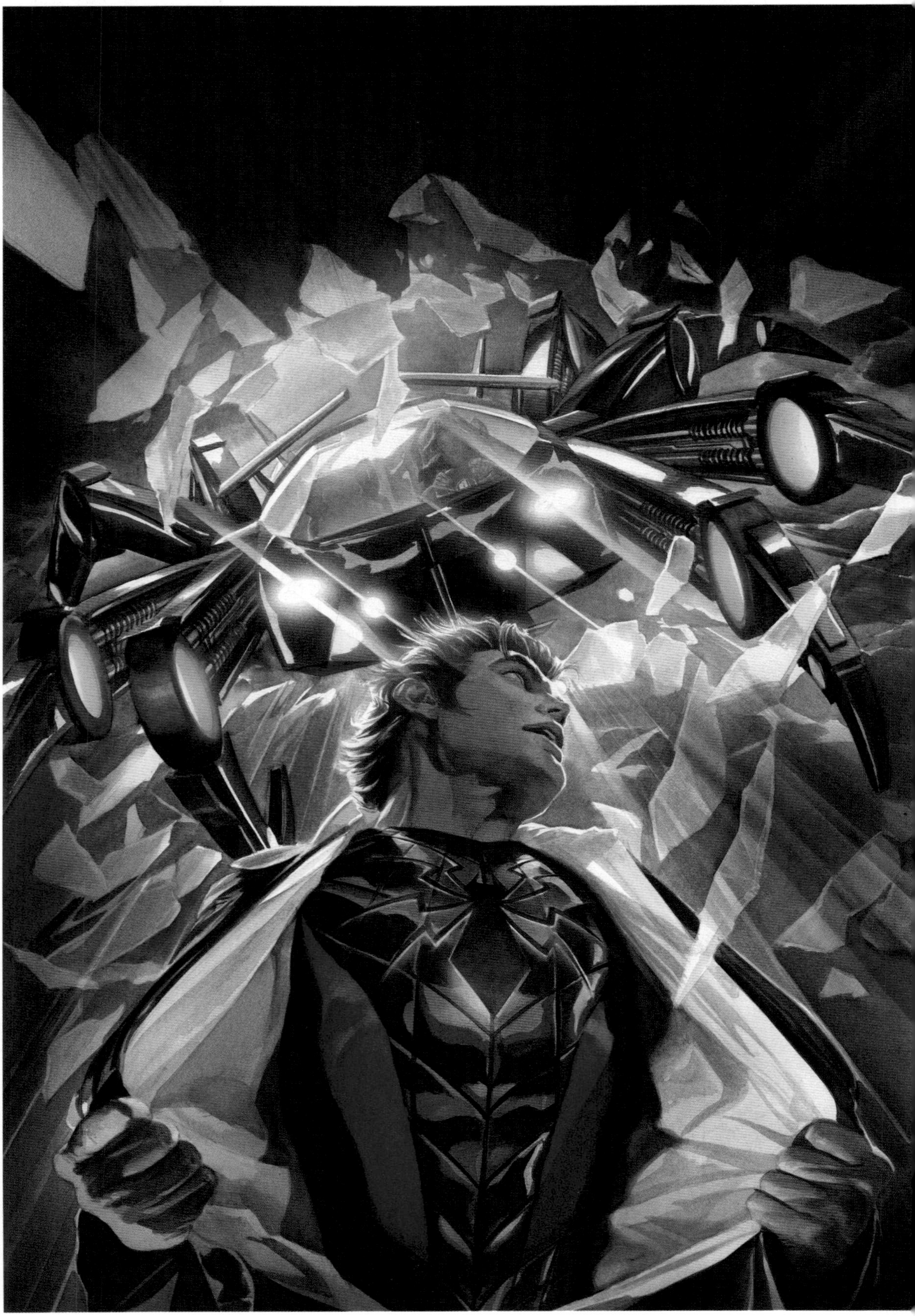

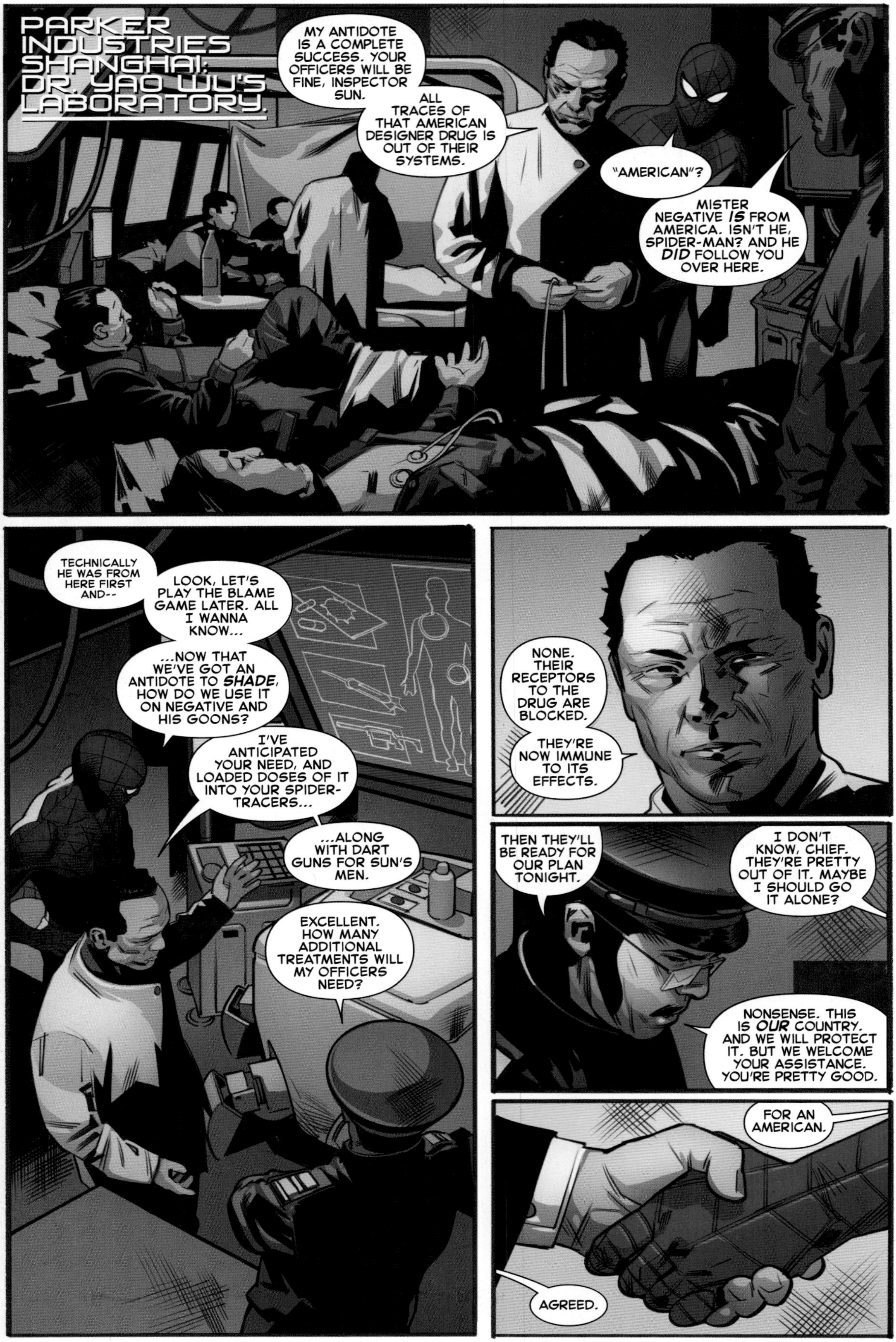
PARKER INDUSTRIES SHANGHAI: DR. YAO WU'S LABORATORY.
MY ANTIDOTE IS A COMPLETE SUCCESS. YOUR OFFICERS WILL BE FINE, INSPECTOR SUN.
ALL TRACES OF THAT AMERICAN DESIGNER DRUG IS OUT OF THEIR SYSTEMS.
"AMERICAN"?
MISTER NEGATIVE IS FROM AMERICA. ISN'T HE, SPIDER-MAN? AND HE DID FOLLOW YOU OVER HERE.
TECHNICALLY HE WAS FROM HERE FIRST AND--
LOOK, LET'S PLAY THE BLAME GAME LATER. ALL I WANNA KNOW...
...NOW THAT WE'VE GOT AN ANTIDOTE TO SHADE, HOW DO WE USE IT ON NEGATIVE AND HIS GOONS?
I'VE ANTICIPATED YOUR NEED, AND LOADED DOSES OF IT INTO YOUR SPIDER-TRACERS...
...ALONG WITH DART GUNS FOR SUN'S MEN.
EXCELLENT. HOW MANY ADDITIONAL TREATMENTS WILL MY OFFICERS NEED?
NONE. THEIR RECEPTORS TO THE DRUG ARE BLOCKED.
THEY'RE NOW IMMUNE TO ITS EFFECTS.
THEN THEY'LL BE READY FOR OUR PLAN TONIGHT.
I DON'T KNOW, CHIEF. THEY'RE PRETTY OUT OF IT. MAYBE I SHOULD GO IT ALONE?
NONSENSE. THIS IS OUR COUNTRY. AND WE WILL PROTECT IT. BUT WE WELCOME YOUR ASSISTANCE. YOU'RE PRETTY GOOD.
FOR AN AMERICAN.
AGREED.

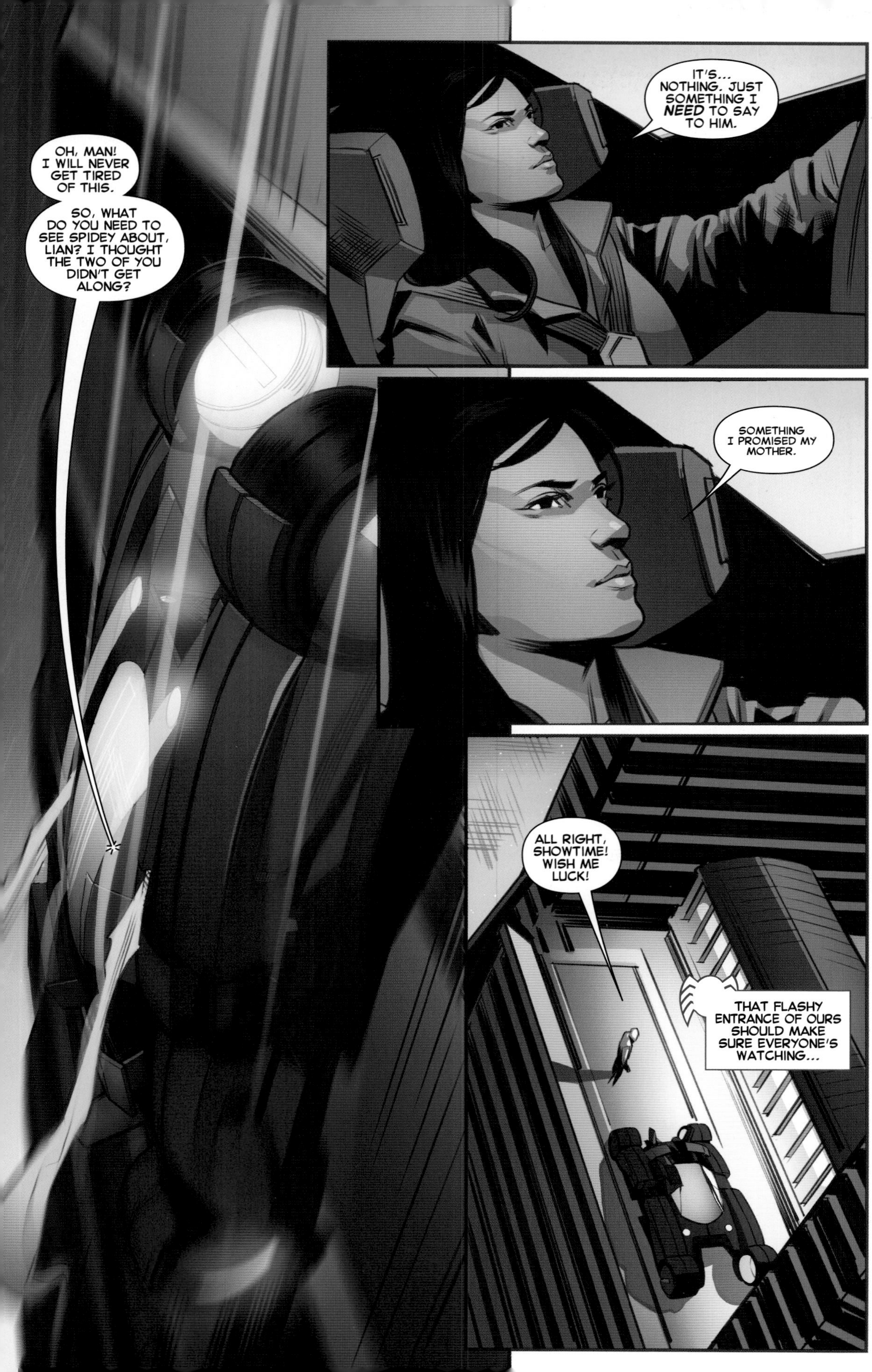
OH, MAN! I WILL NEVER GET TIRED OF THIS.
SO, WHAT DO YOU NEED TO SEE SPIDEY ABOUT, LIAN? I THOUGHT THE TWO OF YOU DIDN'T GET ALONG?
IT'S... NOTHING. JUST SOMETHING I NEED TO SAY TO HIM.
SOMETHING I PROMISED MY MOTHER.
ALL RIGHT, SHOWTIME! WISH ME LUCK!
THAT FLASHY ENTRANCE OF OURS SHOULD MAKE SURE EVERYONE'S WATCHING...

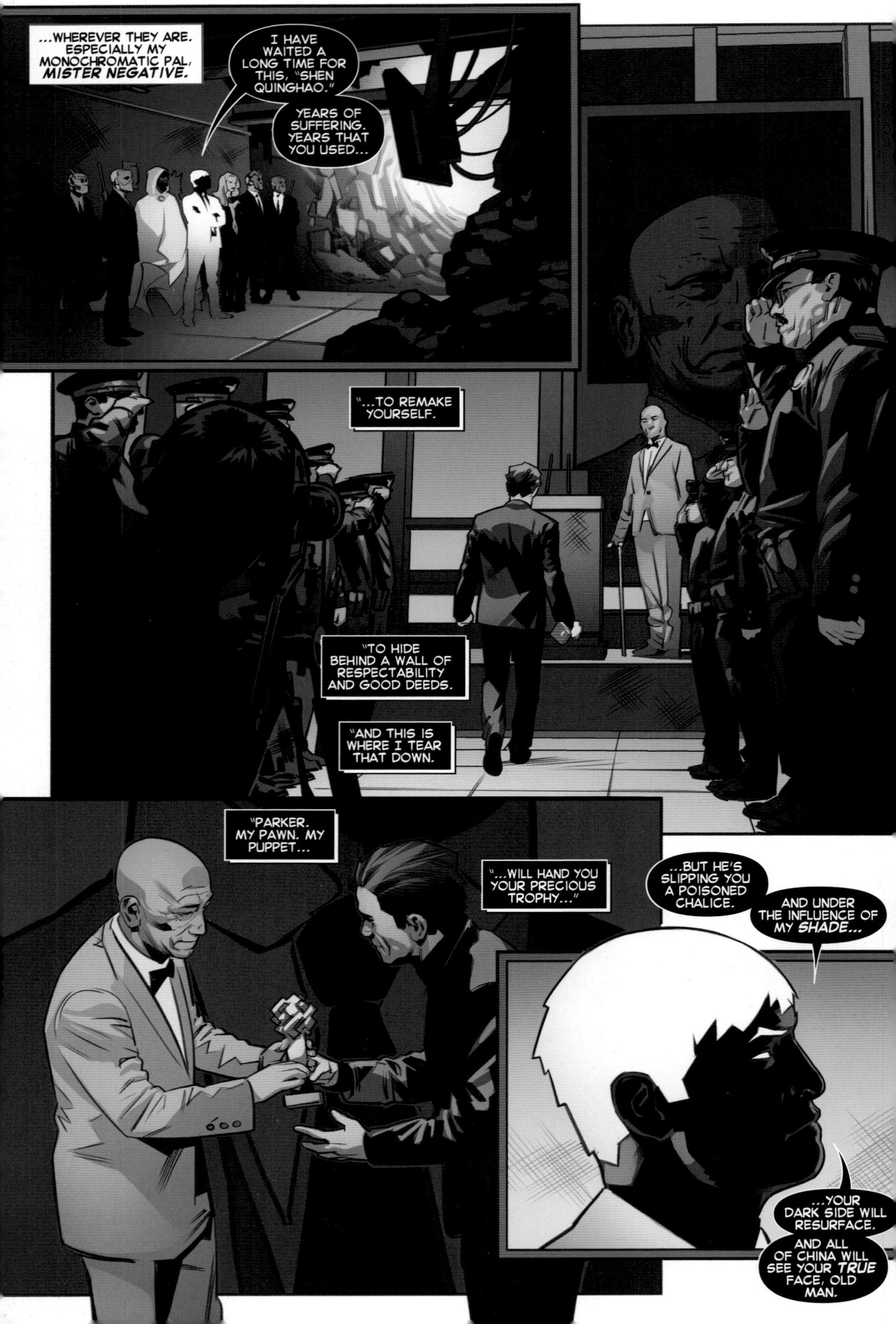
...WHEREVER THEY ARE. ESPECIALLY MY MONOCHROMATIC PAL, *MISTER NEGATIVE.*
I HAVE WAITED A LONG TIME FOR THIS, "SHEN QUINGHAO."
YEARS OF SUFFERING. YEARS THAT YOU USED...
"...TO REMAKE YOURSELF.
"TO HIDE BEHIND A WALL OF RESPECTABILITY AND GOOD DEEDS.
"AND THIS IS WHERE I TEAR THAT DOWN.
"PARKER. MY PAWN. MY PUPPET...
"...WILL HAND YOU YOUR PRECIOUS TROPHY..."
...BUT HE'S SLIPPING YOU A POISONED CHALICE.
AND UNDER THE INFLUENCE OF MY *SHADE...*
...YOUR DARK SIDE WILL RESURFACE.
AND ALL OF CHINA WILL SEE YOUR *TRUE* FACE, OLD MAN.

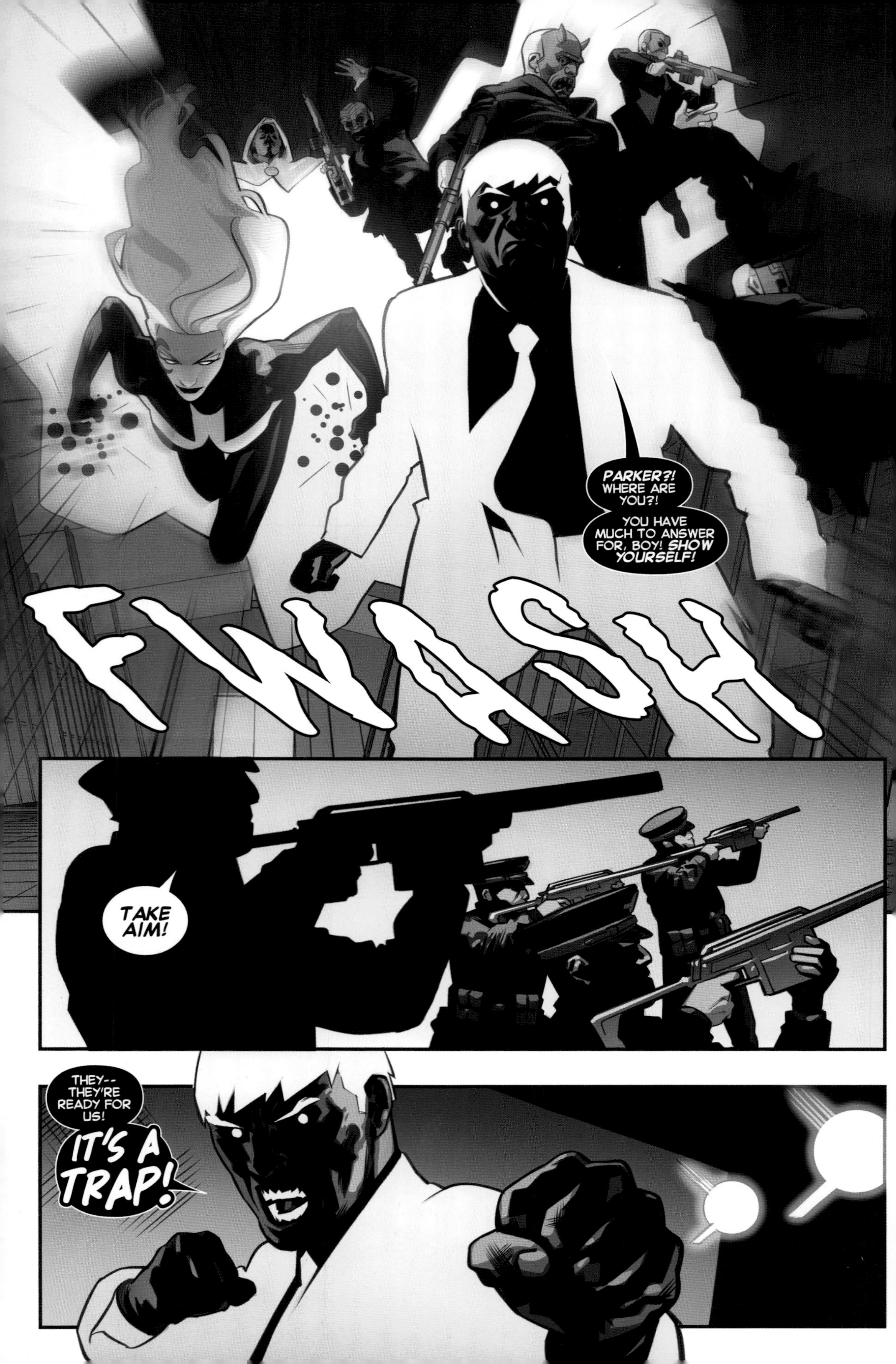
PARKER?! WHERE ARE YOU?!
YOU HAVE MUCH TO ANSWER FOR, BOY! SHOW YOURSELF!
FWASH
TAKE AIM!
THEY-- THEY'RE READY FOR US!
IT'S A TRAP!

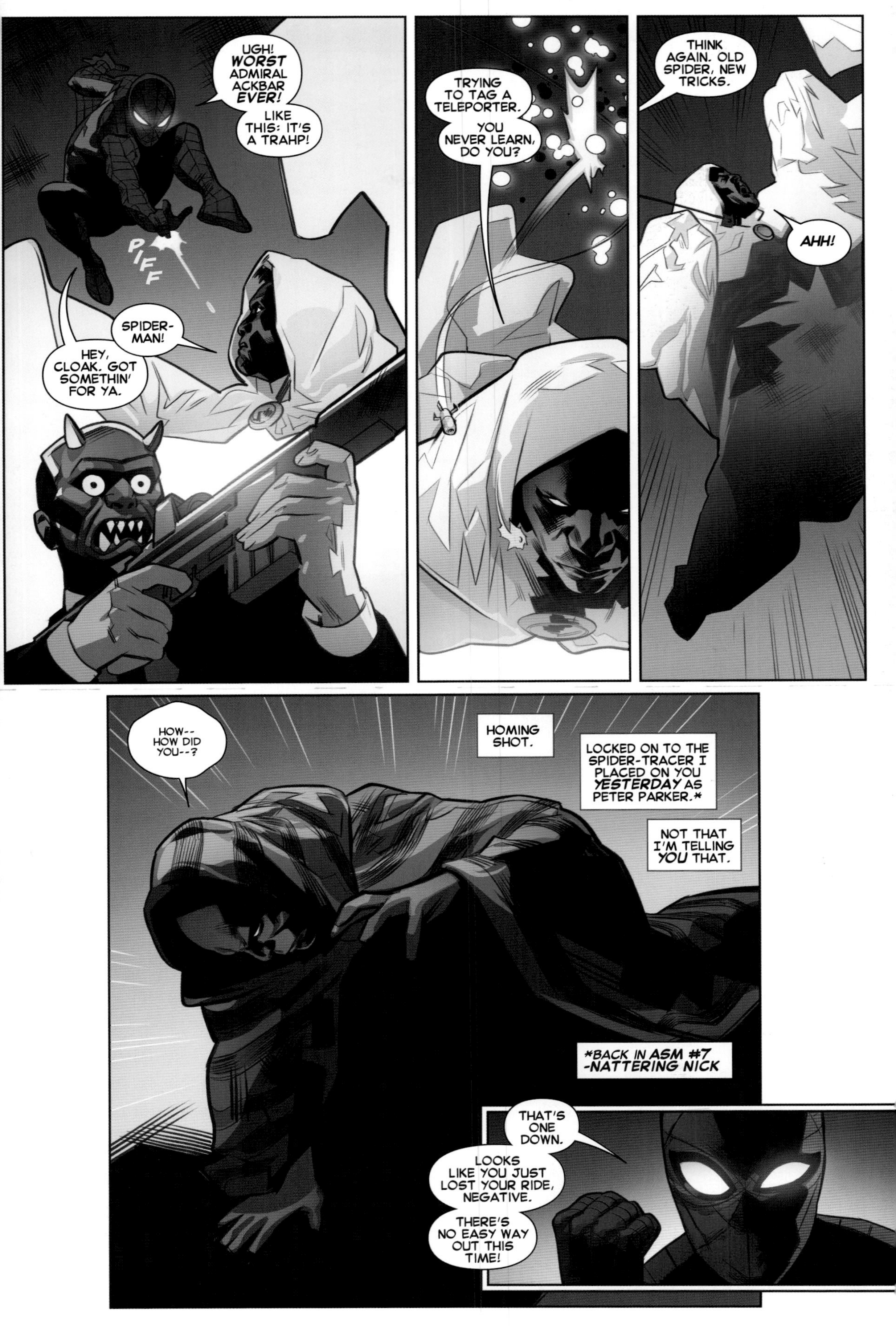
UGH! WORST ADMIRAL ACKBAR EVER!
LIKE THIS: IT'S A TRAHP!
PIFF
SPIDER-MAN!
HEY, CLOAK. GOT SOMETHIN' FOR YA.
TRYING TO TAG A TELEPORTER.
YOU NEVER LEARN, DO YOU?
THINK AGAIN. OLD SPIDER, NEW TRICKS.
AHH!
HOW--HOW DID YOU--?
HOMING SHOT.
LOCKED ON TO THE SPIDER-TRACER I PLACED ON YOU YESTERDAY AS PETER PARKER.*
NOT THAT I'M TELLING YOU THAT.
*BACK IN ASM #7 -NATTERING NICK
THAT'S ONE DOWN.
LOOKS LIKE YOU JUST LOST YOUR RIDE, NEGATIVE.
THERE'S NO EASY WAY OUT THIS TIME!

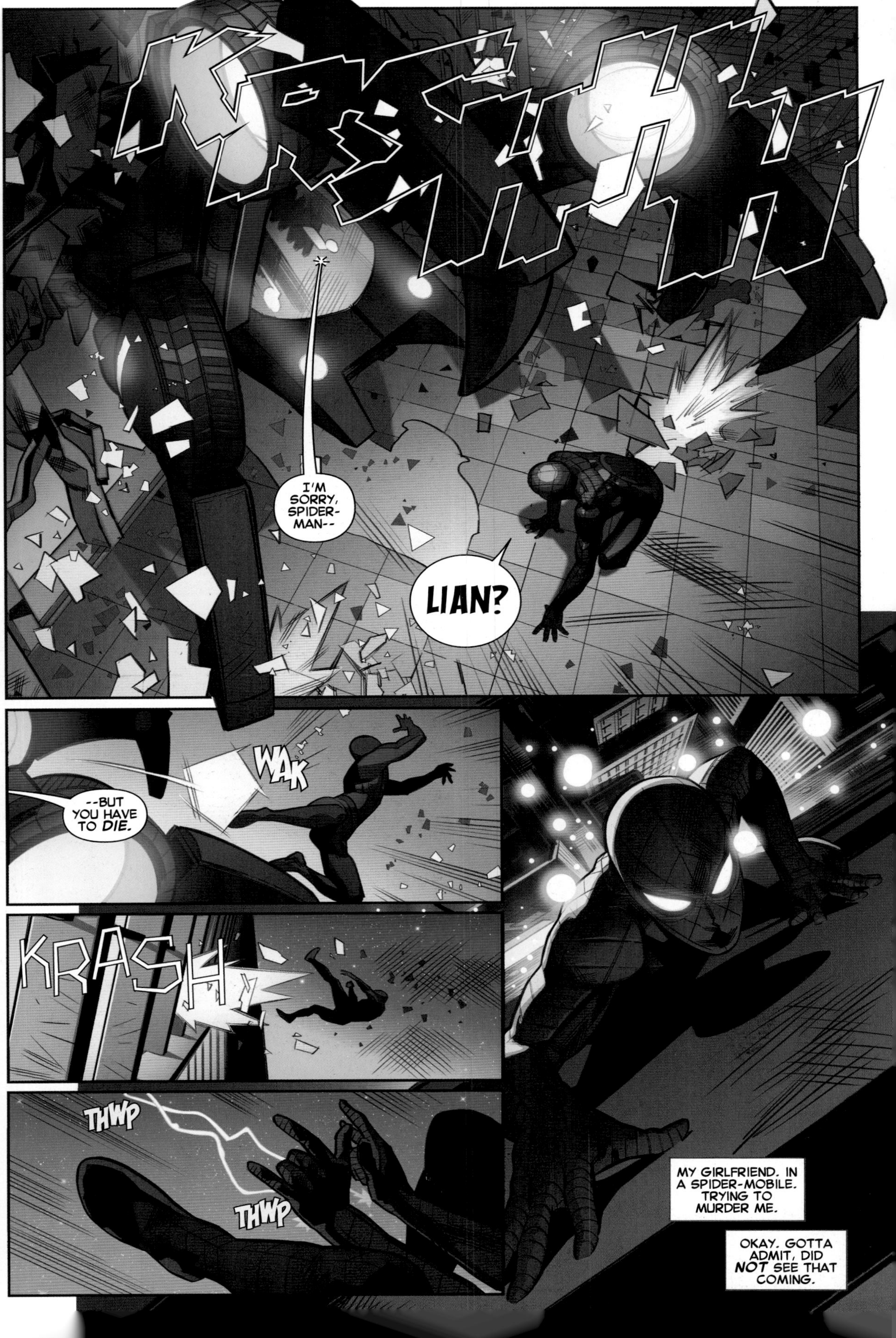
I'M SORRY, SPIDER-MAN--
LIAN?
WAK
--BUT YOU HAVE TO *DIE.*
KRASH
THWP
THWP
MY GIRLFRIEND. IN A SPIDER-MOBILE. TRYING TO MURDER ME.
OKAY. GOTTA ADMIT, DID ***NOT*** SEE THAT COMING.

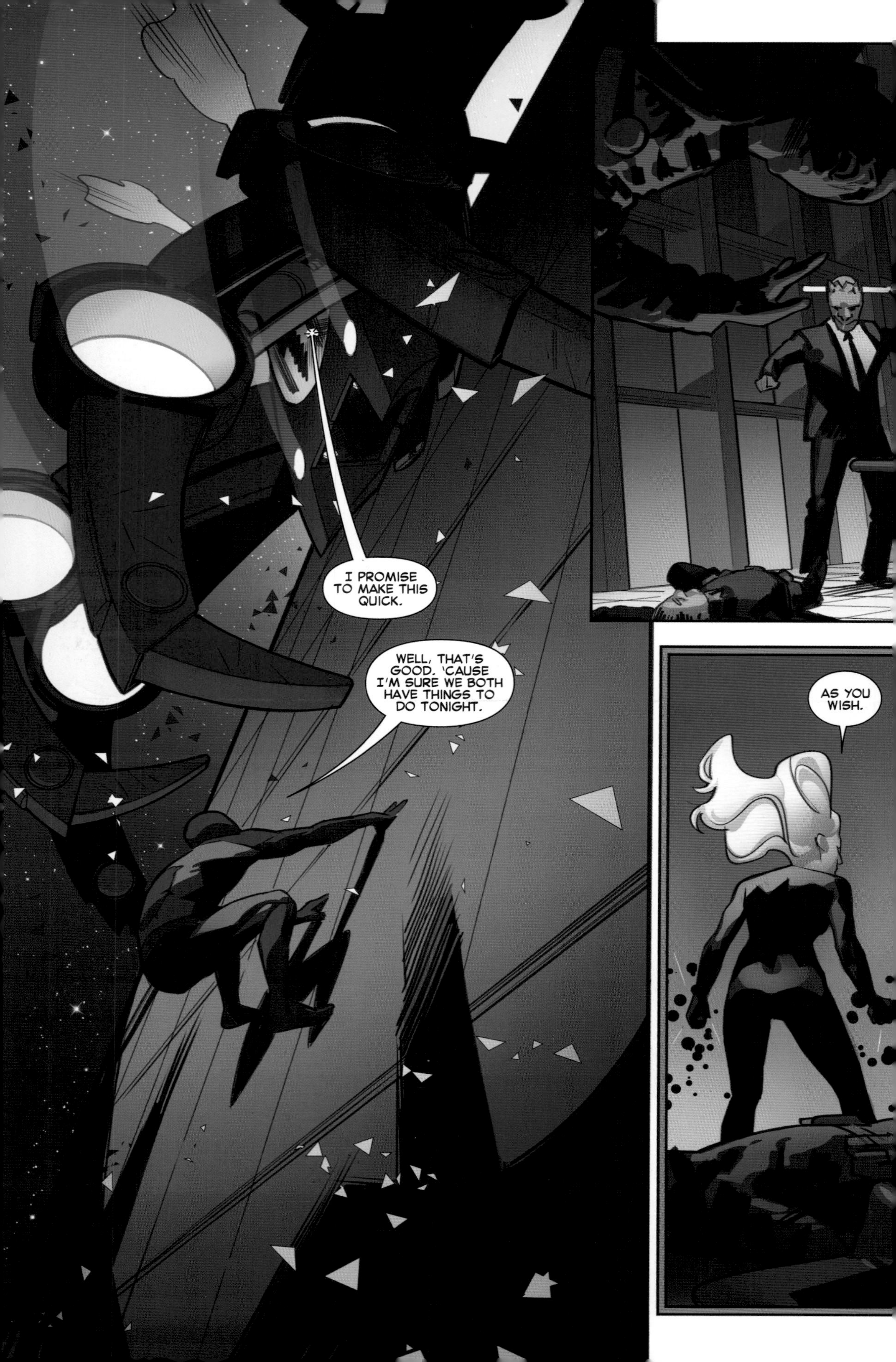
I PROMISE TO MAKE THIS QUICK.
WELL, THAT'S GOOD. 'CAUSE I'M SURE WE BOTH HAVE THINGS TO DO TONIGHT.
AS YOU WISH.

CHANGE OF PLANS. NO SUBTLETY. NO ELABORATE REVENGE.

EVERYONE, KILL THE OLD MAN!

HAVE TO STOP YOU, FOR YOUR OWN SAKE. OR YOU'D NEVER FORGIVE YOURSELF.

LET GO!

TANDY? PLEASE! THIS ISN'T YOU!

DAGGER? WHAT HAVE I DONE?!

ARGH!

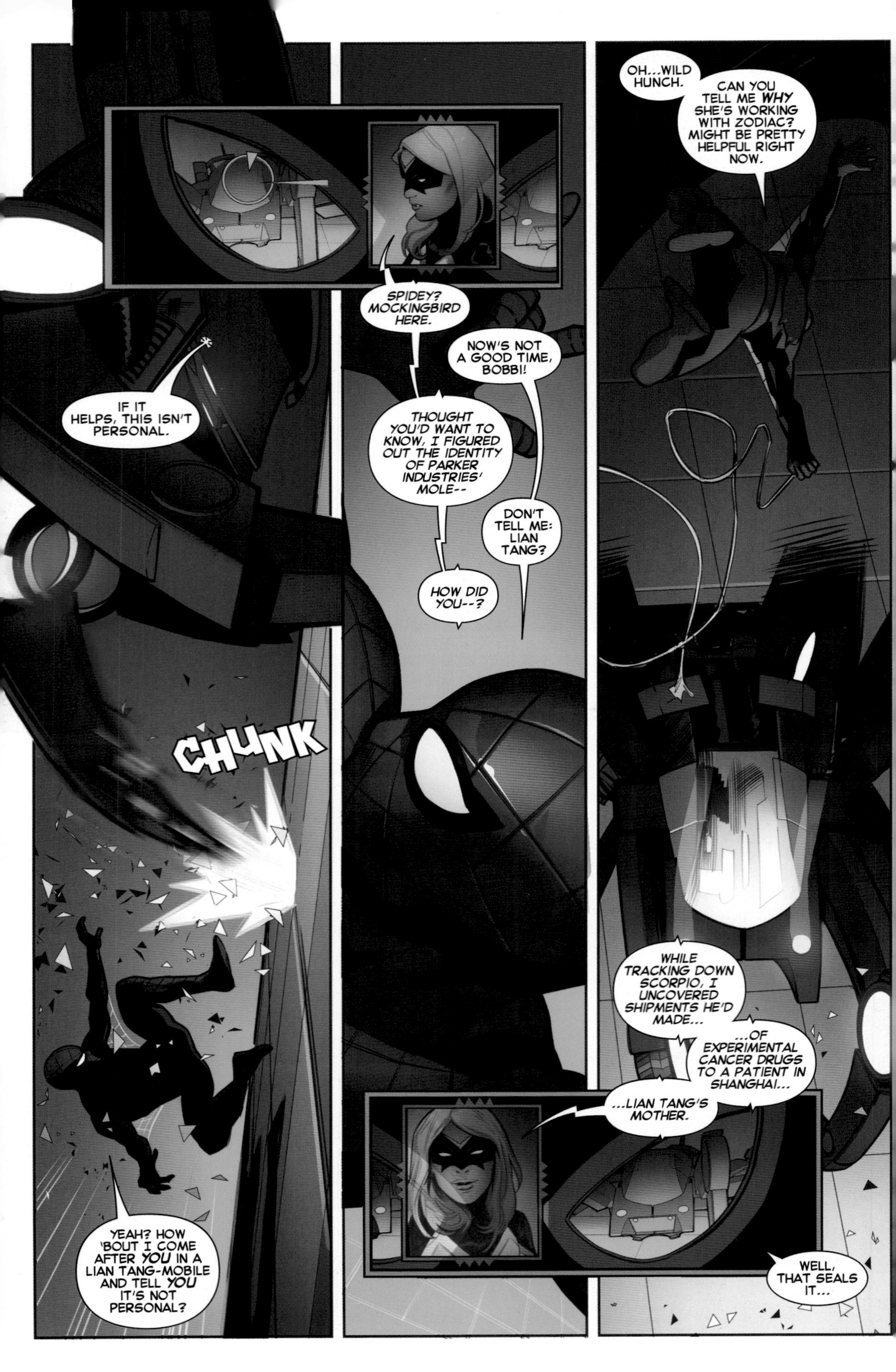
SPIDEY? MOCKINGBIRD HERE.
NOW'S NOT A GOOD TIME, BOBBI!
IF IT HELPS, THIS ISN'T PERSONAL.
THOUGHT YOU'D WANT TO KNOW, I FIGURED OUT THE IDENTITY OF PARKER INDUSTRIES' MOLE--
DON'T TELL ME: LIAN TANG?
HOW DID YOU--?
CHUNK
YEAH? HOW 'BOUT I COME AFTER YOU IN A LIAN TANG-MOBILE AND TELL YOU IT'S NOT PERSONAL?
OH...WILD HUNCH.
CAN YOU TELL ME WHY SHE'S WORKING WITH ZODIAC? MIGHT BE PRETTY HELPFUL RIGHT NOW.
WHILE TRACKING DOWN SCORPIO, I UNCOVERED SHIPMENTS HE'D MADE...
...OF EXPERIMENTAL CANCER DRUGS TO A PATIENT IN SHANGHAI...
...LIAN TANG'S MOTHER.
WELL, THAT SEALS IT...

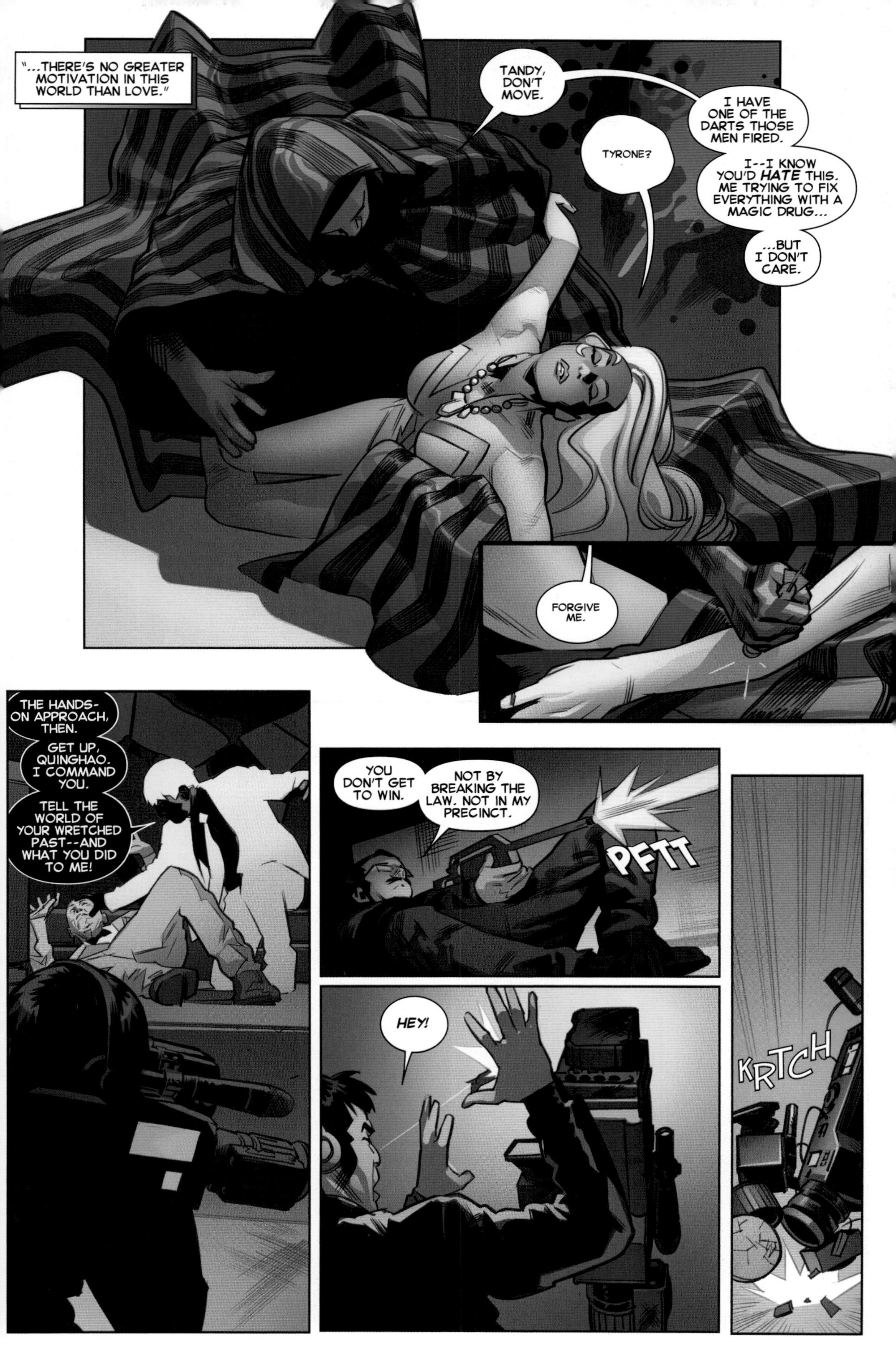
"...THERE'S NO GREATER MOTIVATION IN THIS WORLD THAN LOVE."
TANDY, DON'T MOVE.
TYRONE?
I HAVE ONE OF THE DARTS THOSE MEN FIRED.
I--I KNOW YOU'D HATE THIS. ME TRYING TO FIX EVERYTHING WITH A MAGIC DRUG...
...BUT I DON'T CARE.
FORGIVE ME.
THE HANDS-ON APPROACH, THEN.
GET UP, QUINGHAO. I COMMAND YOU.
TELL THE WORLD OF YOUR WRETCHED PAST--AND WHAT YOU DID TO ME!
YOU DON'T GET TO WIN.
NOT BY BREAKING THE LAW. NOT IN MY PRECINCT.
PFTT
HEY!
KRTCH

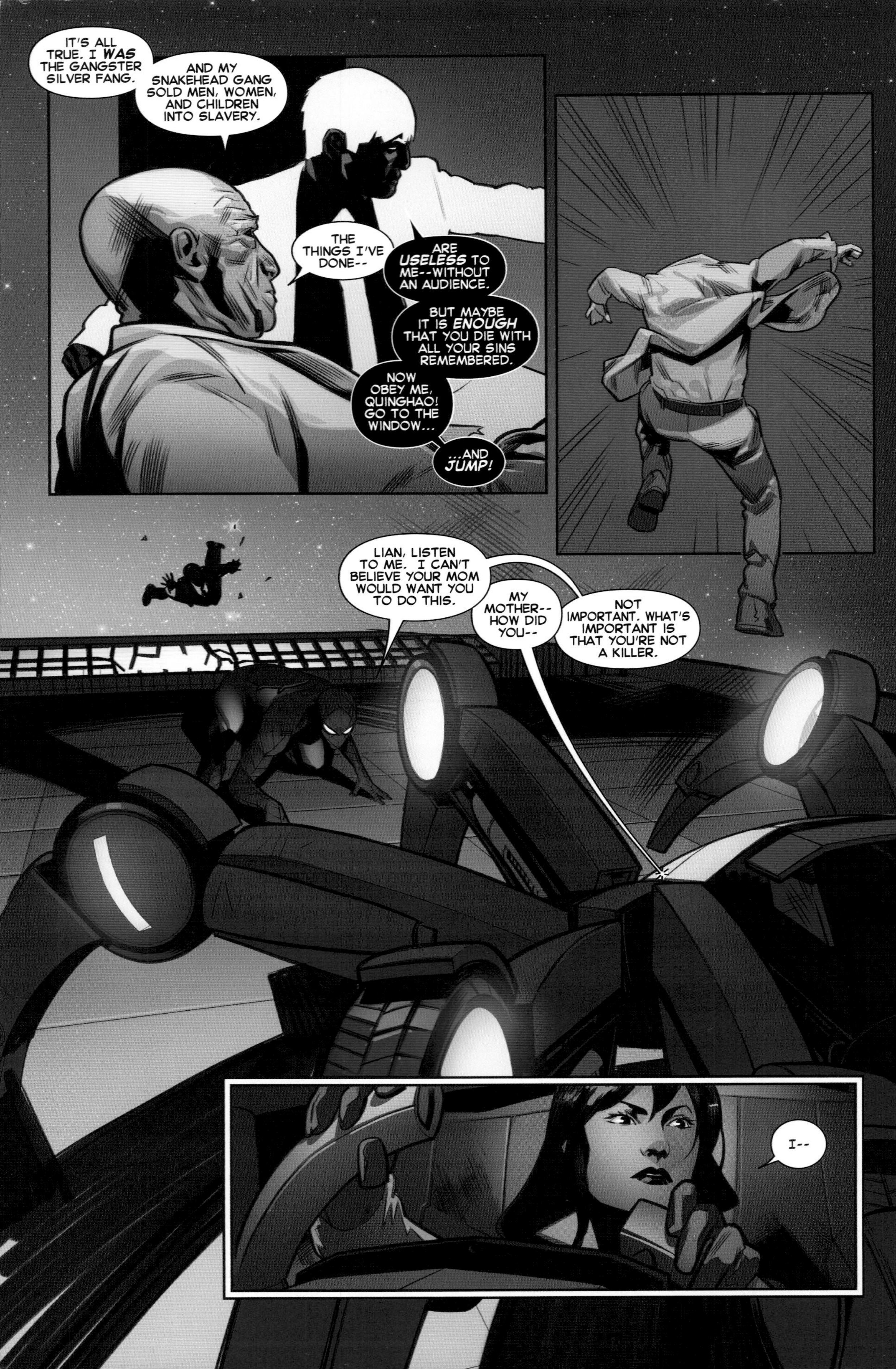
IT'S ALL TRUE. I WAS THE GANGSTER SILVER FANG.
AND MY SNAKEHEAD GANG SOLD MEN, WOMEN, AND CHILDREN INTO SLAVERY.
THE THINGS I'VE DONE--
ARE USELESS TO ME--WITHOUT AN AUDIENCE.
BUT MAYBE IT IS ENOUGH THAT YOU DIE WITH ALL YOUR SINS REMEMBERED.
NOW OBEY ME, QUINGHAO! GO TO THE WINDOW...
...AND JUMP!
LIAN, LISTEN TO ME. I CAN'T BELIEVE YOUR MOM WOULD WANT YOU TO DO THIS.
MY MOTHER-- HOW DID YOU--
NOT IMPORTANT. WHAT'S IMPORTANT IS THAT YOU'RE NOT A KILLER.
I--

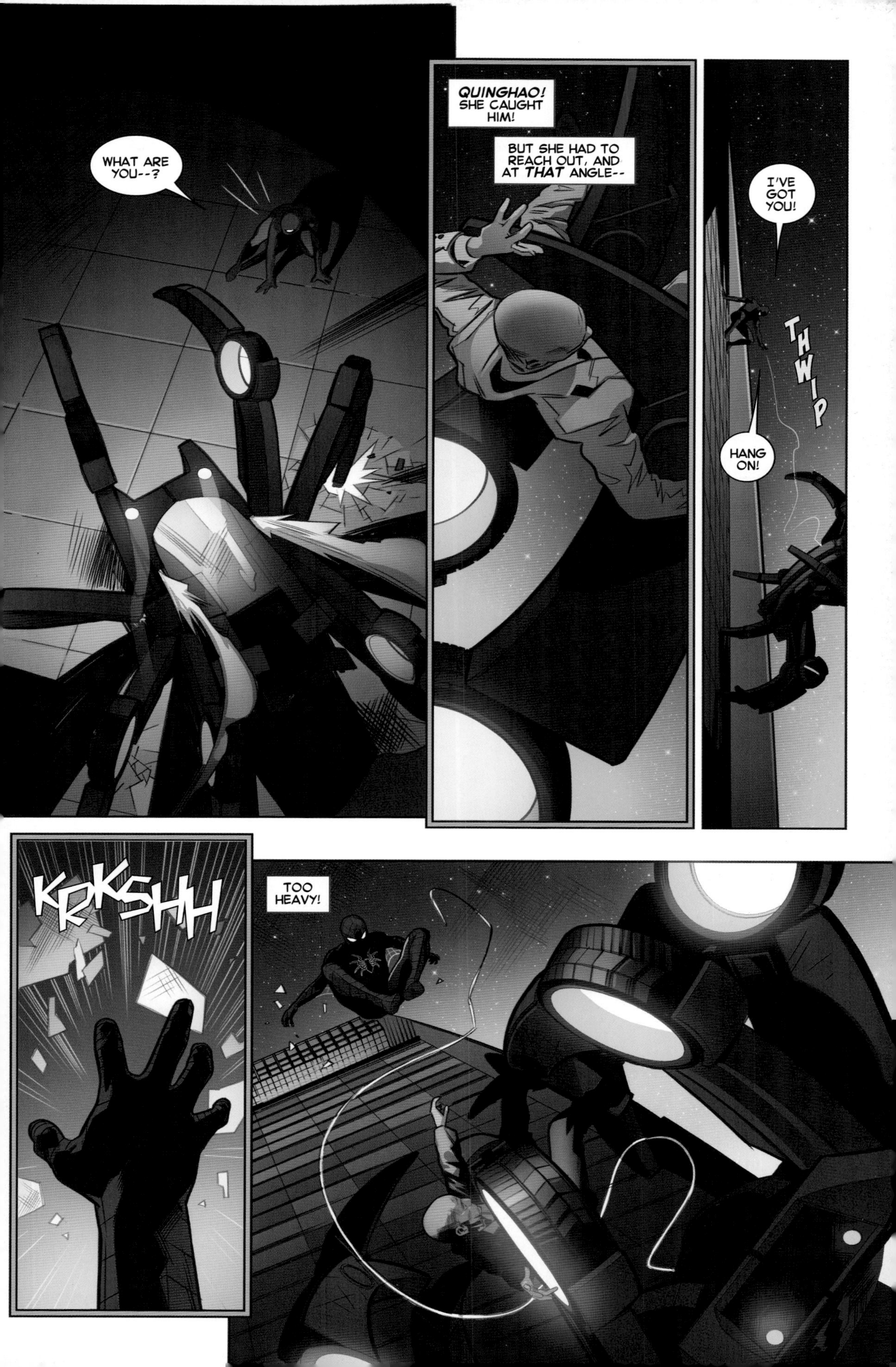
WHAT ARE YOU--?
QUINGHAO! SHE CAUGHT HIM!
BUT SHE HAD TO REACH OUT, AND AT THAT ANGLE--
I'VE GOT YOU!
THWIP
HANG ON!
KRKSHH
TOO HEAVY!

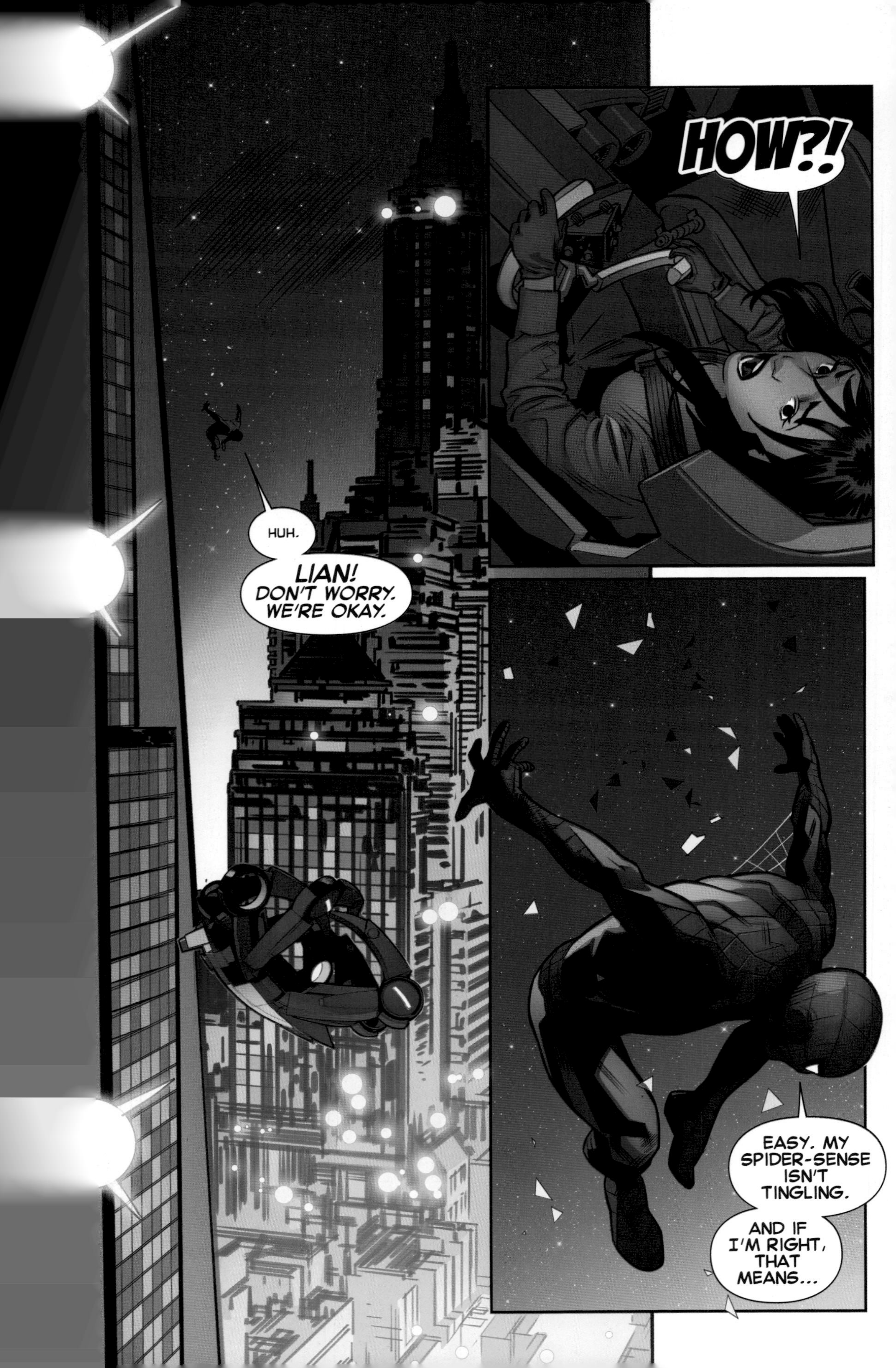
HOW?!
HUH.
LIAN! DON'T WORRY. WE'RE OKAY.
EASY. MY SPIDER-SENSE ISN'T TINGLING.
AND IF I'M RIGHT, THAT MEANS...

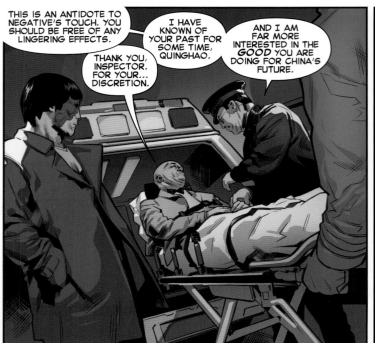

THIS IS AN ANTIDOTE TO NEGATIVE'S TOUCH. YOU SHOULD BE FREE OF ANY LINGERING EFFECTS.

THANK YOU, INSPECTOR. FOR YOUR... DISCRETION.

I HAVE KNOWN OF YOUR PAST FOR SOME TIME, QUINGHAO.

AND I AM FAR MORE INTERESTED IN THE *GOOD* YOU ARE DOING FOR CHINA'S FUTURE.

YOU ARE A LUCKY MAN, QUINGHAO. SOME OF US CARRY OUR MISTAKES WITH US FOR ALL TO SEE. MAYBE THAT'S HOW IT SHOULD BE.

I WON'T BE SHARING MY HARD WORK WITH A MAN LIKE YOU.

GOODBYE, SHEN.

WHAT HAPPENS TO ME NOW?

I'M FIRED? GOING TO JAIL? WHAT? JUST TELL ME MOTHER WILL BE--

LIAN, STOP...

I GAVE ZODIAC OUR SECURITY CODES. I TRIED TO *KILL* YOU. I--

I UNDERSTAND.

I KNOW WHAT IT MEANS TO RISK EVERYTHING TO HELP FAMILY. SO DOES PETER.

WE'D BE HYPOCRITES IF WE DIDN'T GIVE YOU A CHANCE...

...TO *WORK* WITH US. WE'RE GOING TO HELP YOUR MOM. AND YOU'RE GOING HELP US TAKE DOWN ZODIAC.

I WAS ONLY THEIR MOLE.

FINE. LET'S SEE WHAT YOU CAN "DIG UP" FOR THE GOOD GUYS.

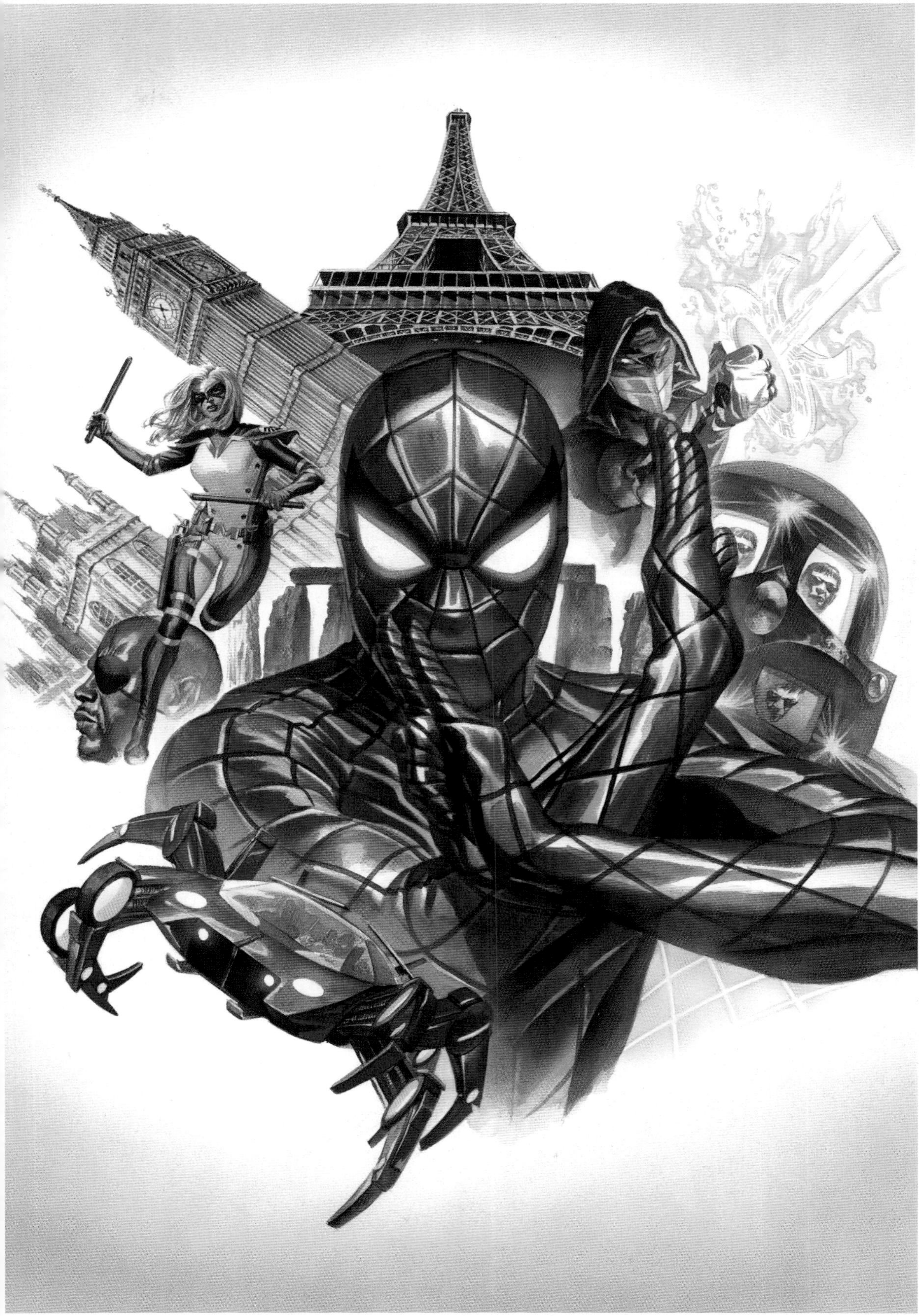

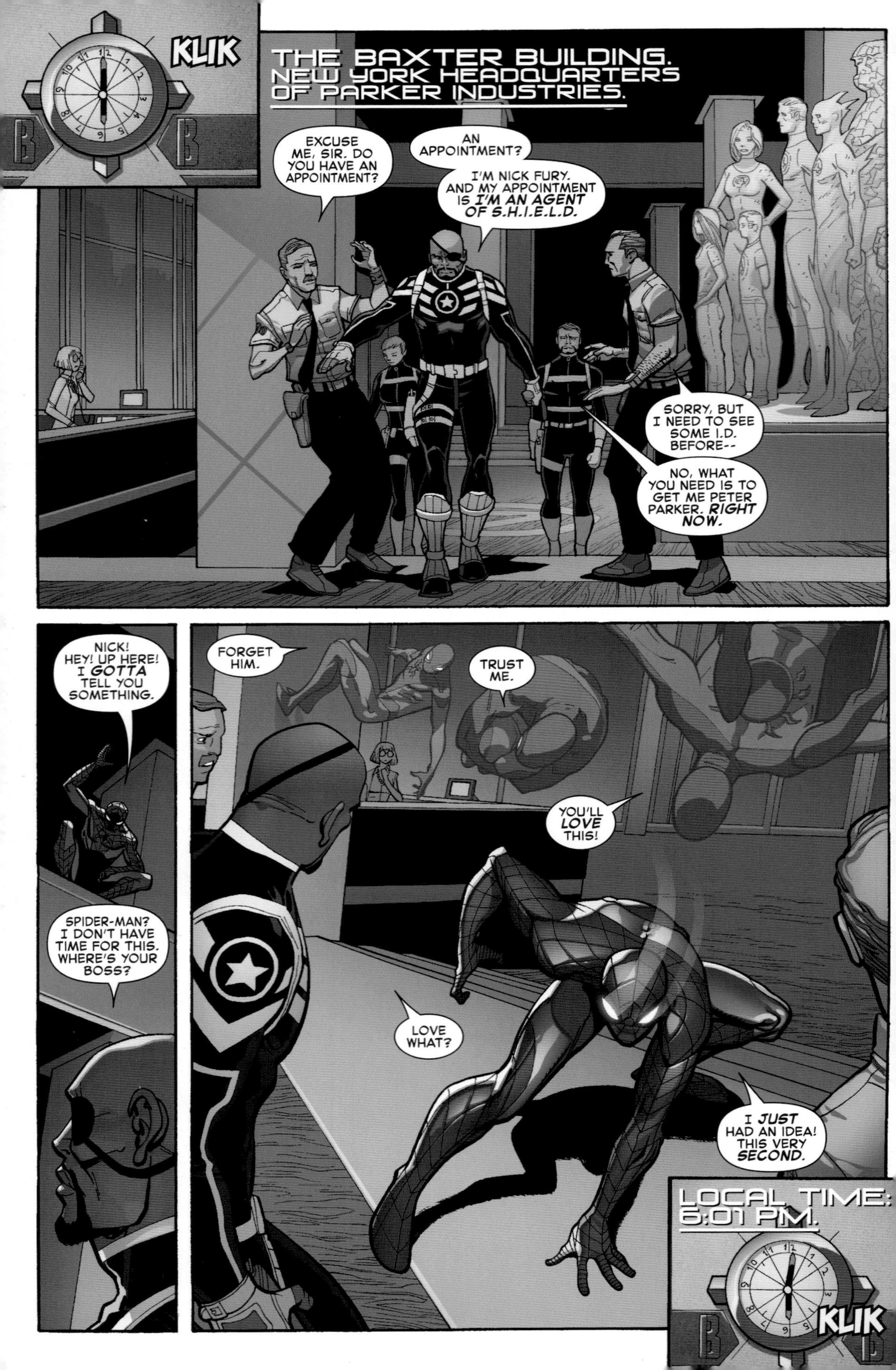
KLIK
THE BAXTER BUILDING.
NEW YORK HEADQUARTERS OF PARKER INDUSTRIES.
EXCUSE ME, SIR. DO YOU HAVE AN APPOINTMENT?
AN APPOINTMENT?
I'M NICK FURY. AND MY APPOINTMENT IS *I'M AN AGENT OF S.H.I.E.L.D.*
SORRY, BUT I NEED TO SEE SOME I.D. BEFORE--
NO, WHAT YOU NEED IS TO GET ME PETER PARKER. *RIGHT NOW.*
NICK! HEY! UP HERE! I *GOTTA* TELL YOU SOMETHING.
SPIDER-MAN? I DON'T HAVE TIME FOR THIS. WHERE'S YOUR BOSS?
FORGET HIM.
TRUST ME.
YOU'LL *LOVE* THIS!
LOVE WHAT?
I *JUST* HAD AN IDEA! THIS VERY *SECOND.*
LOCAL TIME: 6:01 P.M.
KLIK

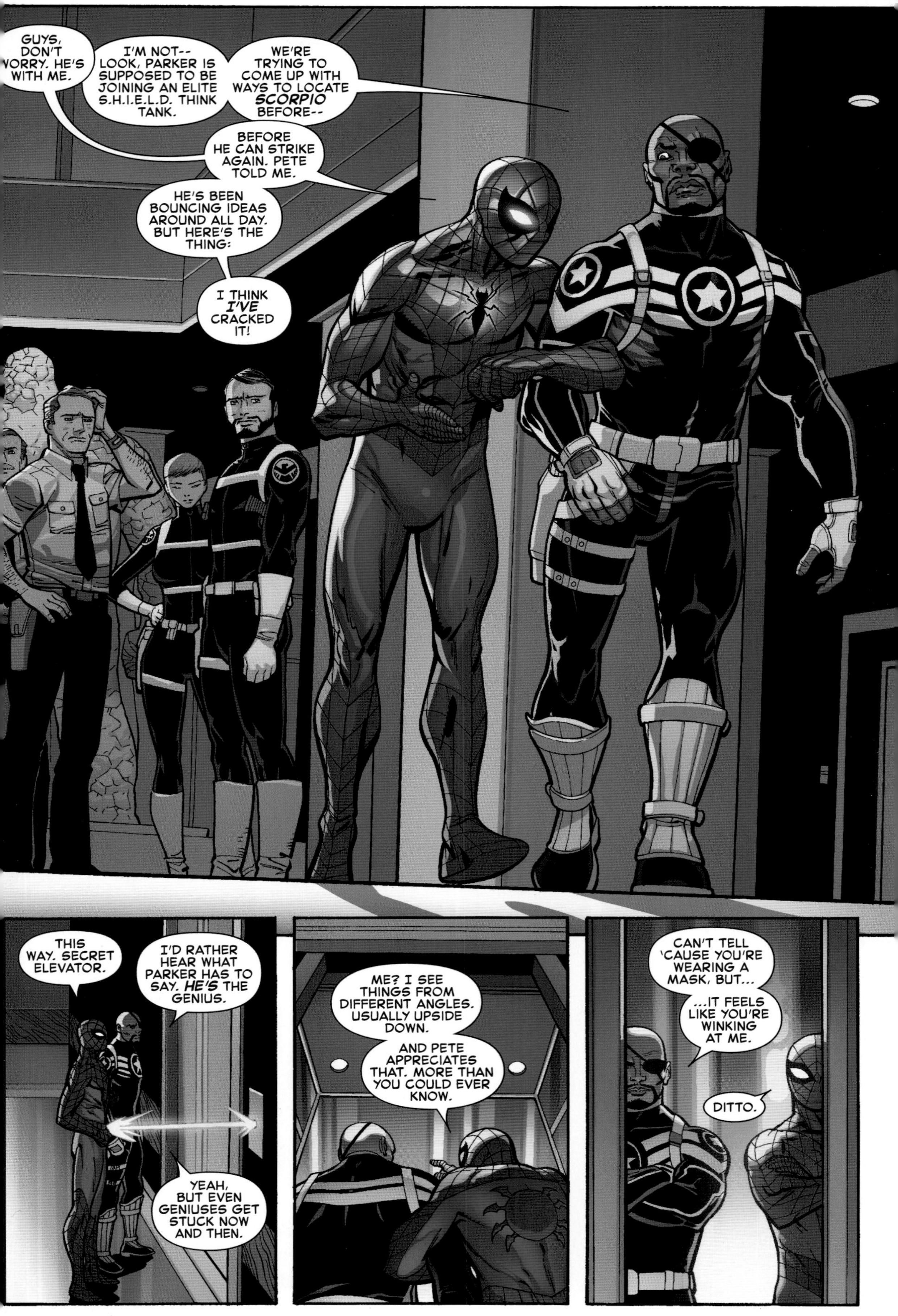
GUYS, DON'T WORRY. HE'S WITH ME.
I'M NOT-- LOOK, PARKER IS SUPPOSED TO BE JOINING AN ELITE S.H.I.E.L.D. THINK TANK.
WE'RE TRYING TO COME UP WITH WAYS TO LOCATE SCORPIO BEFORE--
BEFORE HE CAN STRIKE AGAIN. PETE TOLD ME.
HE'S BEEN BOUNCING IDEAS AROUND ALL DAY. BUT HERE'S THE THING:
I THINK I'VE CRACKED IT!
THIS WAY. SECRET ELEVATOR.
I'D RATHER HEAR WHAT PARKER HAS TO SAY. HE'S THE GENIUS.
YEAH, BUT EVEN GENIUSES GET STUCK NOW AND THEN.
ME? I SEE THINGS FROM DIFFERENT ANGLES. USUALLY UPSIDE DOWN.
AND PETE APPRECIATES THAT. MORE THAN YOU COULD EVER KNOW.
CAN'T TELL 'CAUSE YOU'RE WEARING A MASK, BUT...
...IT FEELS LIKE YOU'RE WINKING AT ME.
DITTO.

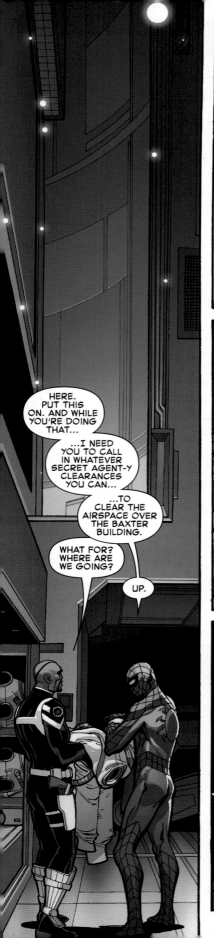

SPACESUITS? YOU'RE KIDDING.

AND--HOW DOES THIS ALREADY HAVE MY INSIGNIA ON IT?

HERE. PUT THIS ON. AND WHILE YOU'RE DOING THAT...

...I NEED YOU TO CALL IN WHATEVER SECRET AGENT-Y CLEARANCES YOU CAN...

...TO CLEAR THE AIRSPACE OVER THE BAXTER BUILDING.

WHAT FOR? WHERE ARE WE GOING?

UP.

YOU LIKE? THEY CAN DO DIGITAL LOGOS ON THE FLY.

ALSO EMOJIS.

WANT TO SWITCH TO EMOJIS? THEN WE'D KNOW EACH OTHER'S MOODS.

OR NOT.

TALK.

FINE. WE'RE GONNA USE S.H.I.E.L.D. *SATELLITES* TO PINPOINT SCORPIO'S POSITION.

IMPOSSIBLE. ZODIAC HACKED OUR SYSTEMS, REMEMBER?

HELL, SCORPIO *STILL* HAS REMOTE CONTROL OVER THEM. WE'RE COMPLETELY SHUT OUT.

I KNOW. HENCE THE CRAZY IDEA. WE'RE GONNA REACTIVATE 'EM...

...MANUALLY.

TO THE ARACHNO-ROCKET!

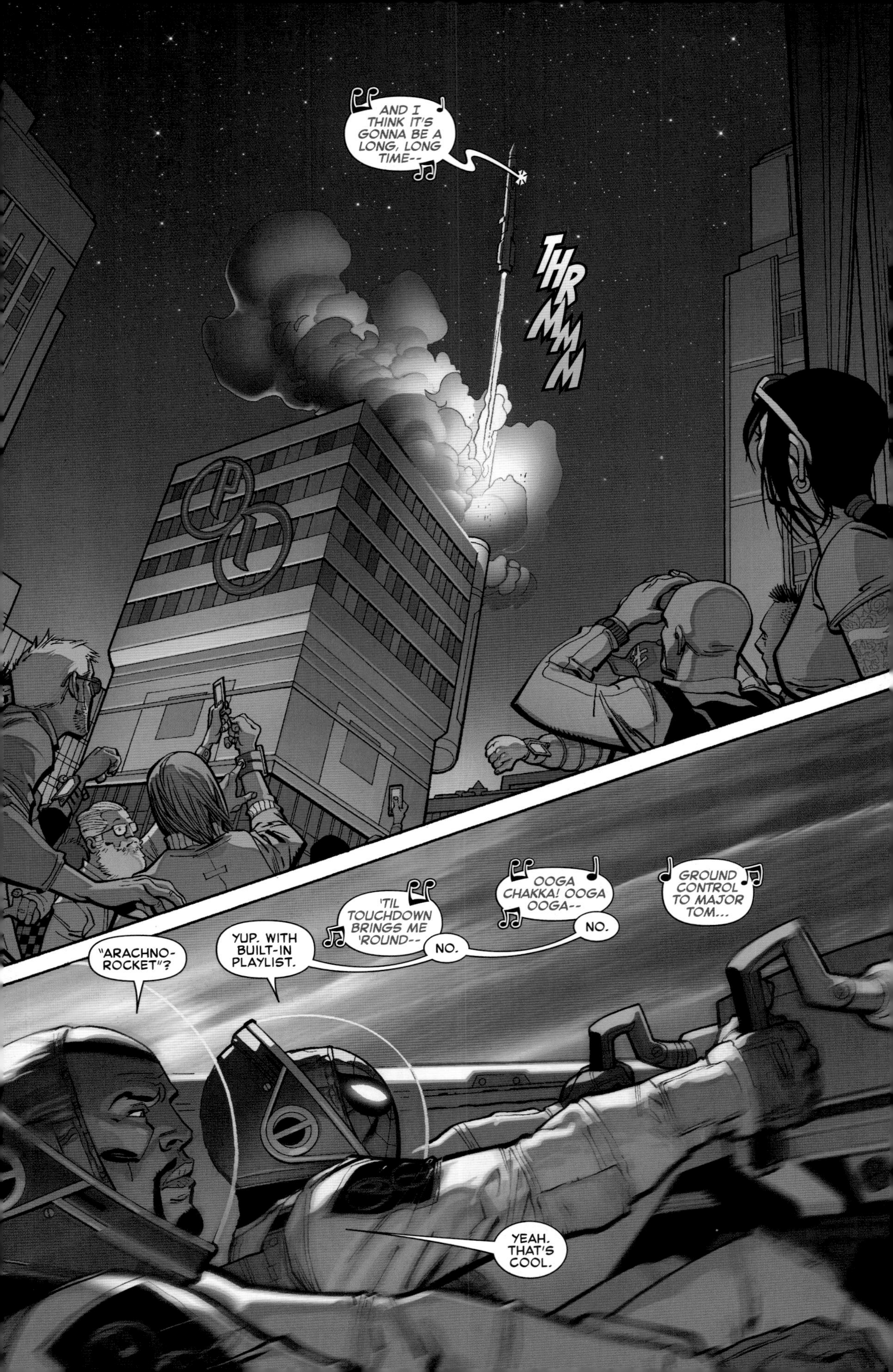
AND I THINK IT'S GONNA BE A LONG, LONG TIME--
THRMMMM
"ARACHNO-ROCKET"?
YUP. WITH BUILT-IN PLAYLIST.
'TIL TOUCHDOWN BRINGS ME 'ROUND--
NO.
OOGA CHAKKA! OOGA OOGA--
NO.
GROUND CONTROL TO MAJOR TOM...
YEAH. THAT'S COOL.

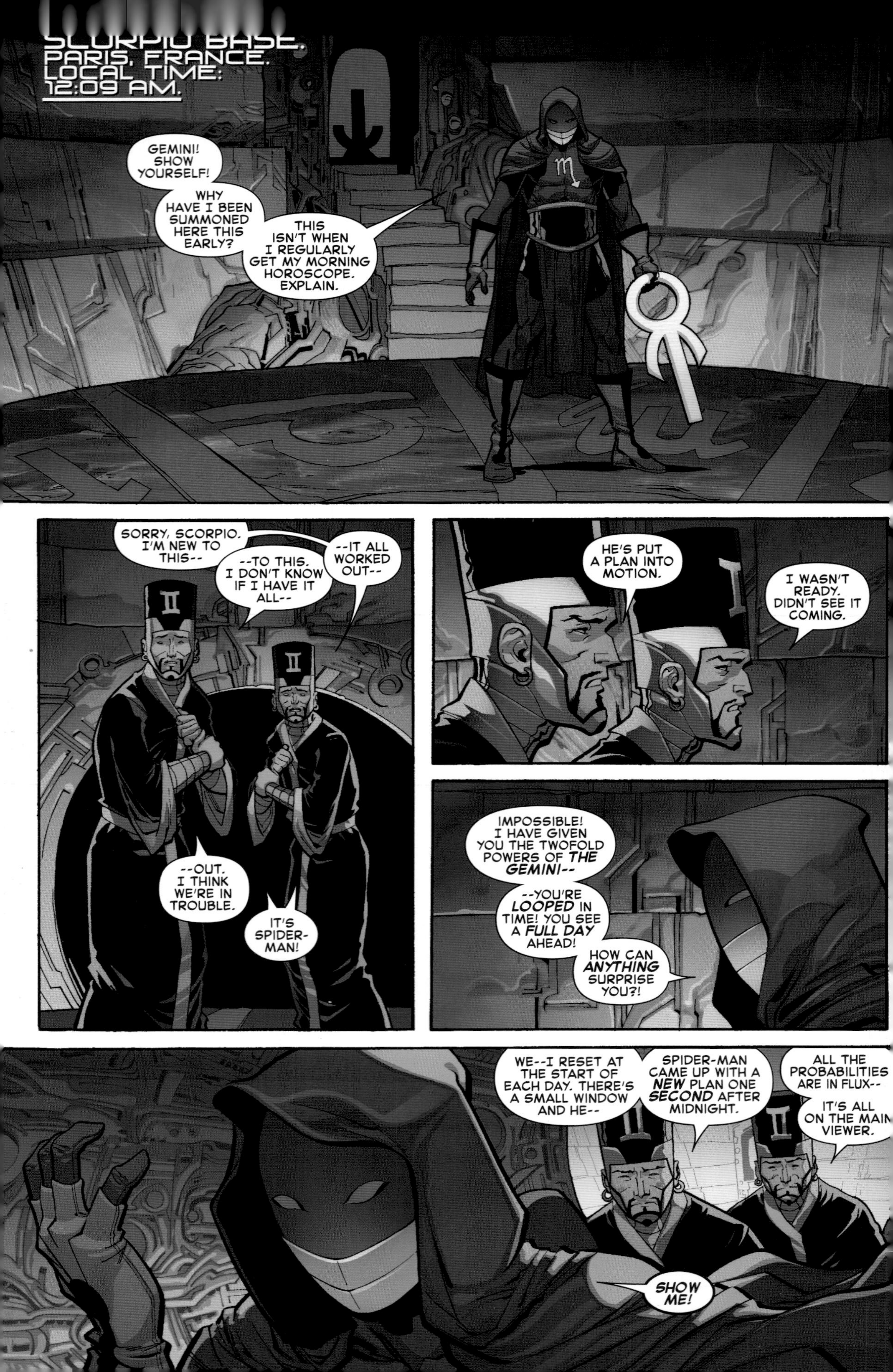
PARIS, FRANCE.
LOCAL TIME:
12:09 AM.
GEMINI! SHOW YOURSELF!
WHY HAVE I BEEN SUMMONED HERE THIS EARLY?
THIS ISN'T WHEN I REGULARLY GET MY MORNING HOROSCOPE. EXPLAIN.
SORRY, SCORPIO. I'M NEW TO THIS--
--TO THIS. I DON'T KNOW IF I HAVE IT ALL--
--IT ALL WORKED OUT--
--OUT. I THINK WE'RE IN TROUBLE.
IT'S SPIDER-MAN!
HE'S PUT A PLAN INTO MOTION.
I WASN'T READY. DIDN'T SEE IT COMING.
IMPOSSIBLE! I HAVE GIVEN YOU THE TWOFOLD POWERS OF THE GEMINI--
--YOU'RE LOOPED IN TIME! YOU SEE A FULL DAY AHEAD!
HOW CAN ANYTHING SURPRISE YOU?!
WE--I RESET AT THE START OF EACH DAY. THERE'S A SMALL WINDOW AND HE--
SPIDER-MAN CAME UP WITH A NEW PLAN ONE SECOND AFTER MIDNIGHT.
ALL THE PROBABILITIES ARE IN FLUX--
IT'S ALL ON THE MAIN VIEWER.
SHOW ME!

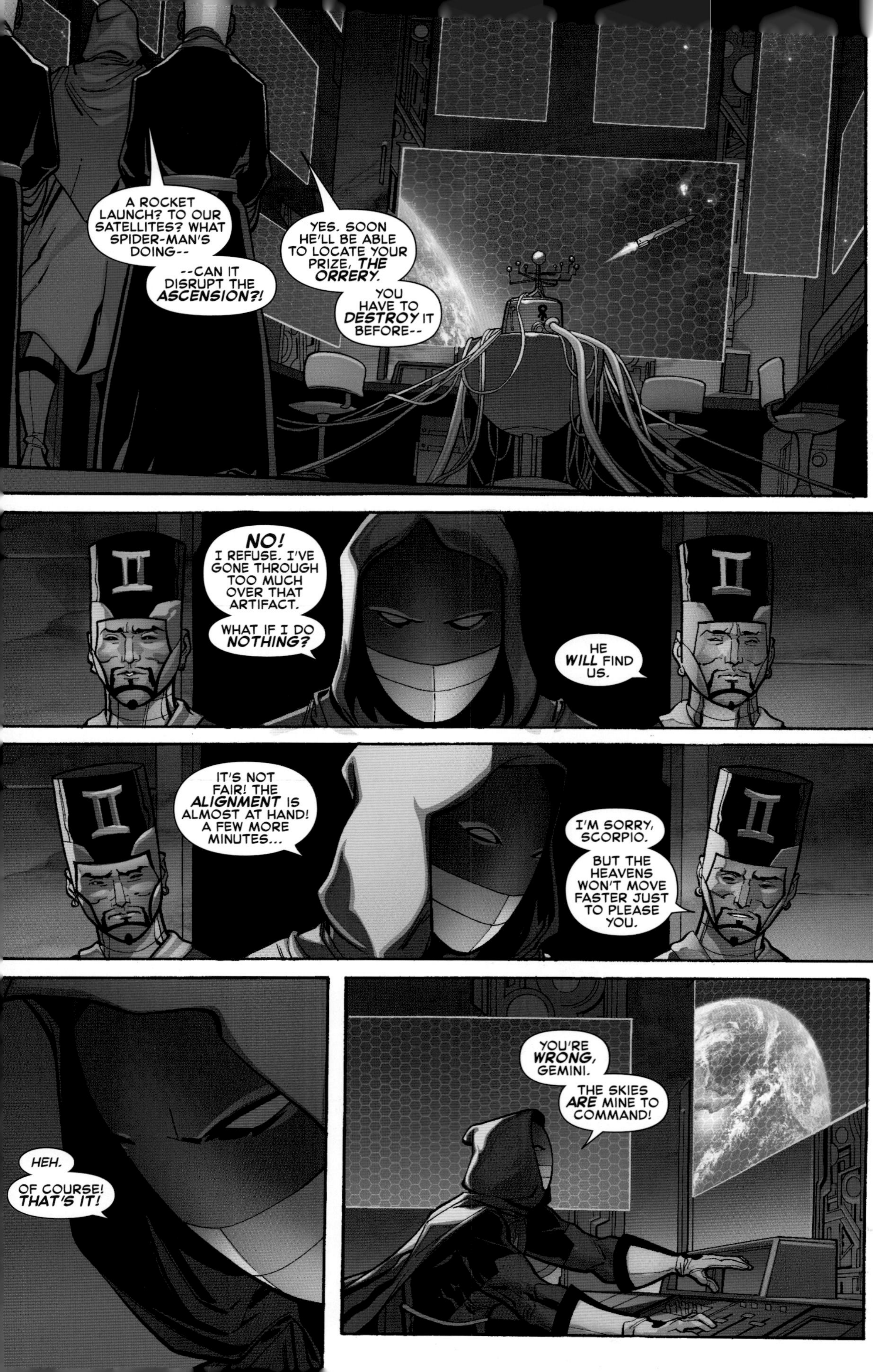
A ROCKET LAUNCH? TO OUR SATELLITES? WHAT SPIDER-MAN'S DOING--
--CAN IT DISRUPT THE ASCENSION?!
YES. SOON HE'LL BE ABLE TO LOCATE YOUR PRIZE, THE ORRERY.
YOU HAVE TO DESTROY IT BEFORE--
NO! I REFUSE. I'VE GONE THROUGH TOO MUCH OVER THAT ARTIFACT.
WHAT IF I DO NOTHING?
HE WILL FIND US.
IT'S NOT FAIR! THE ALIGNMENT IS ALMOST AT HAND! A FEW MORE MINUTES...
I'M SORRY, SCORPIO.
BUT THE HEAVENS WON'T MOVE FASTER JUST TO PLEASE YOU.
HEH.
OF COURSE! THAT'S IT!
YOU'RE WRONG, GEMINI.
THE SKIES ARE MINE TO COMMAND!

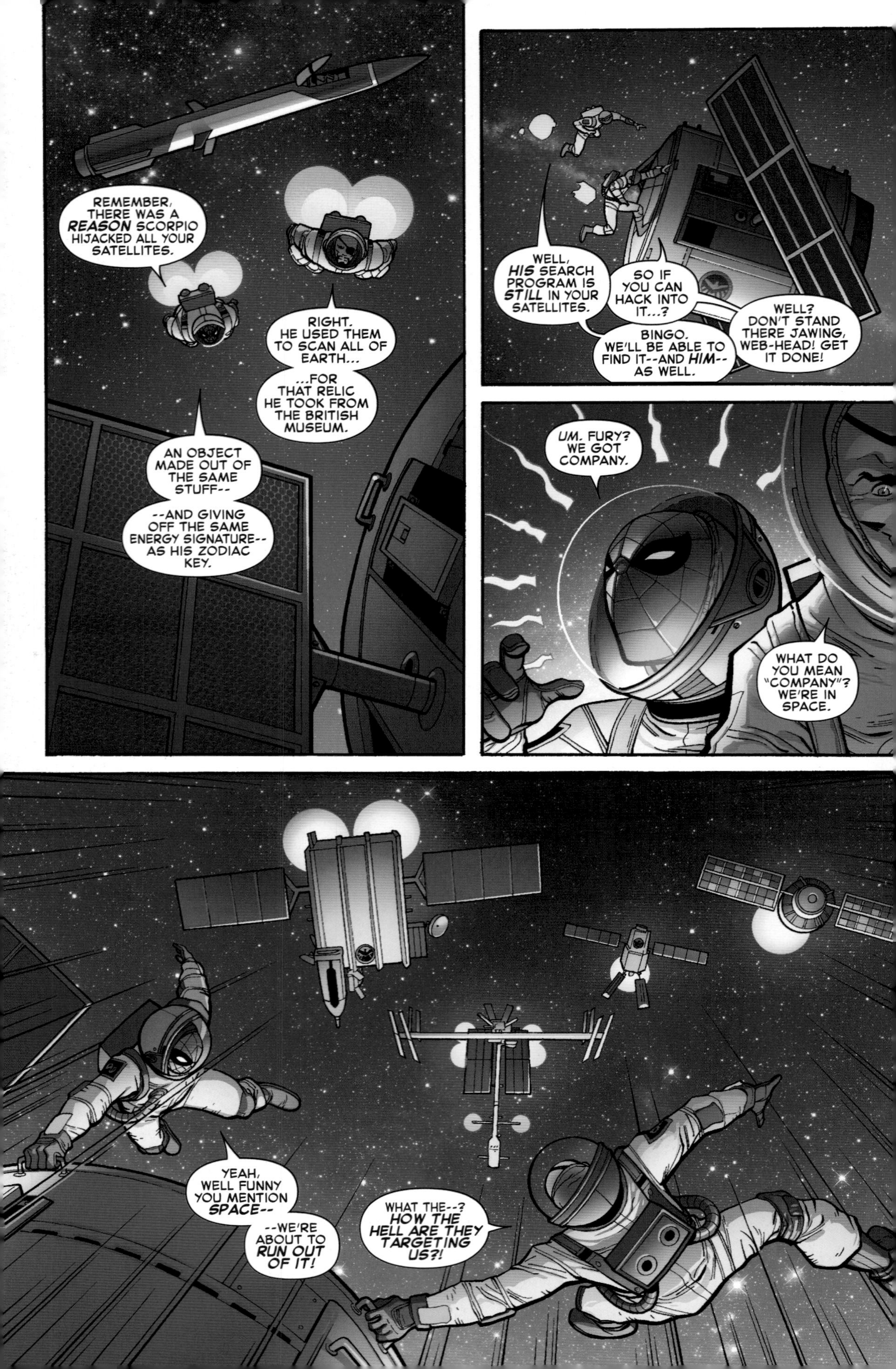
REMEMBER, THERE WAS A REASON SCORPIO HIJACKED ALL YOUR SATELLITES.
RIGHT. HE USED THEM TO SCAN ALL OF EARTH...
...FOR THAT RELIC HE TOOK FROM THE BRITISH MUSEUM.
AN OBJECT MADE OUT OF THE SAME STUFF--
--AND GIVING OFF THE SAME ENERGY SIGNATURE--AS HIS ZODIAC KEY.
WELL, HIS SEARCH PROGRAM IS STILL IN YOUR SATELLITES.
SO IF YOU CAN HACK INTO IT...?
BINGO. WE'LL BE ABLE TO FIND IT--AND HIM--AS WELL.
WELL? DON'T STAND THERE JAWING, WEB-HEAD! GET IT DONE!
UM. FURY? WE GOT COMPANY.
WHAT DO YOU MEAN "COMPANY"? WE'RE IN SPACE.
YEAH, WELL FUNNY YOU MENTION SPACE--
--WE'RE ABOUT TO RUN OUT OF IT!
WHAT THE--? HOW THE HELL ARE THEY TARGETING US?!

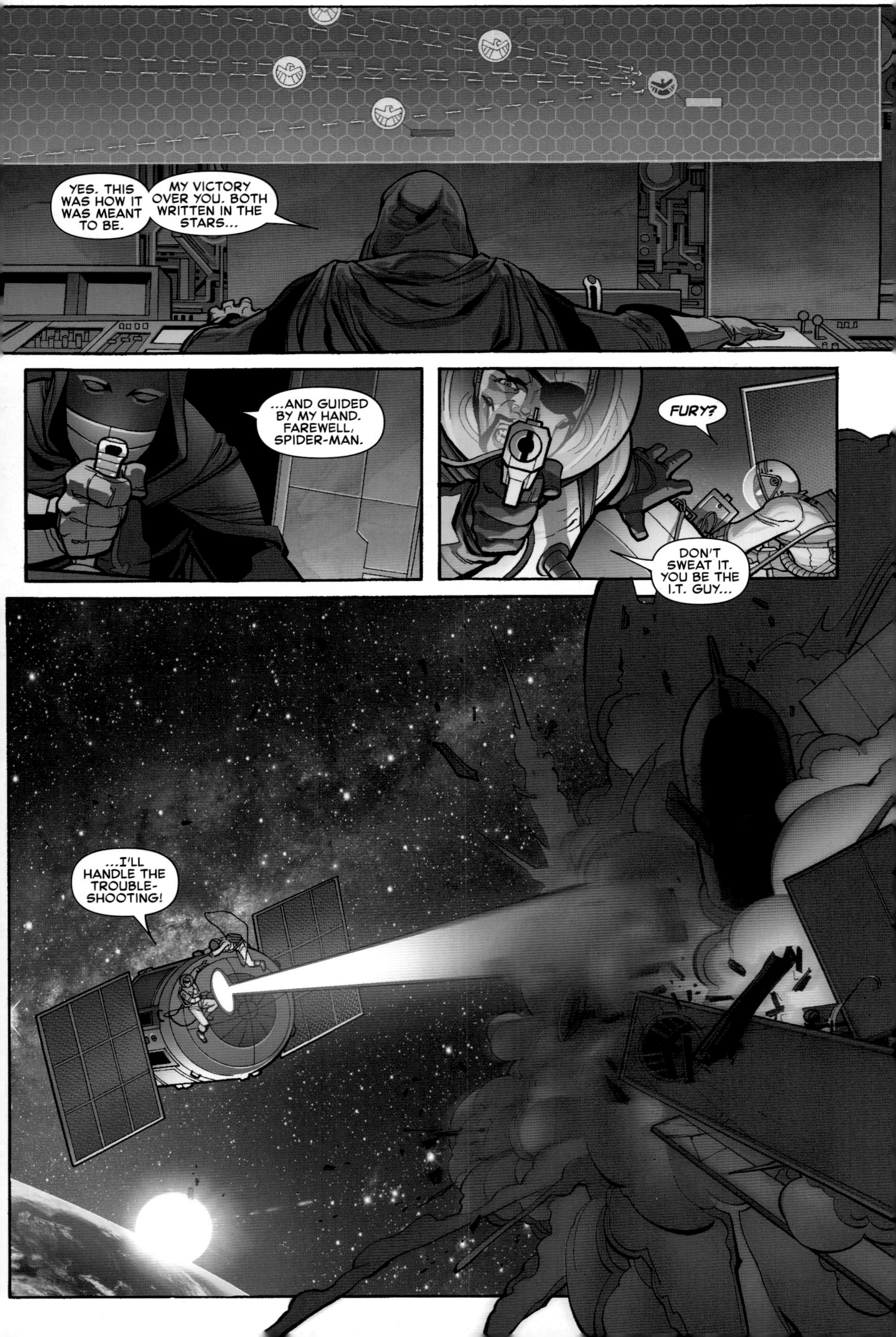
YES. THIS WAS HOW IT WAS MEANT TO BE.
MY VICTORY OVER YOU. BOTH WRITTEN IN THE STARS...
...AND GUIDED BY MY HAND. FAREWELL, SPIDER-MAN.
FURY?
DON'T SWEAT IT. YOU BE THE I.T. GUY...
...I'LL HANDLE THE TROUBLE-SHOOTING!

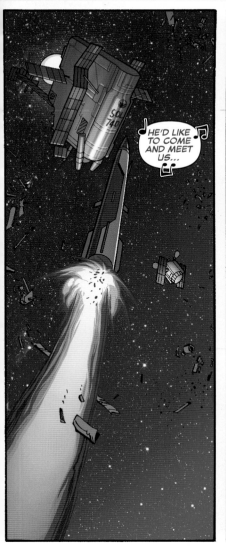

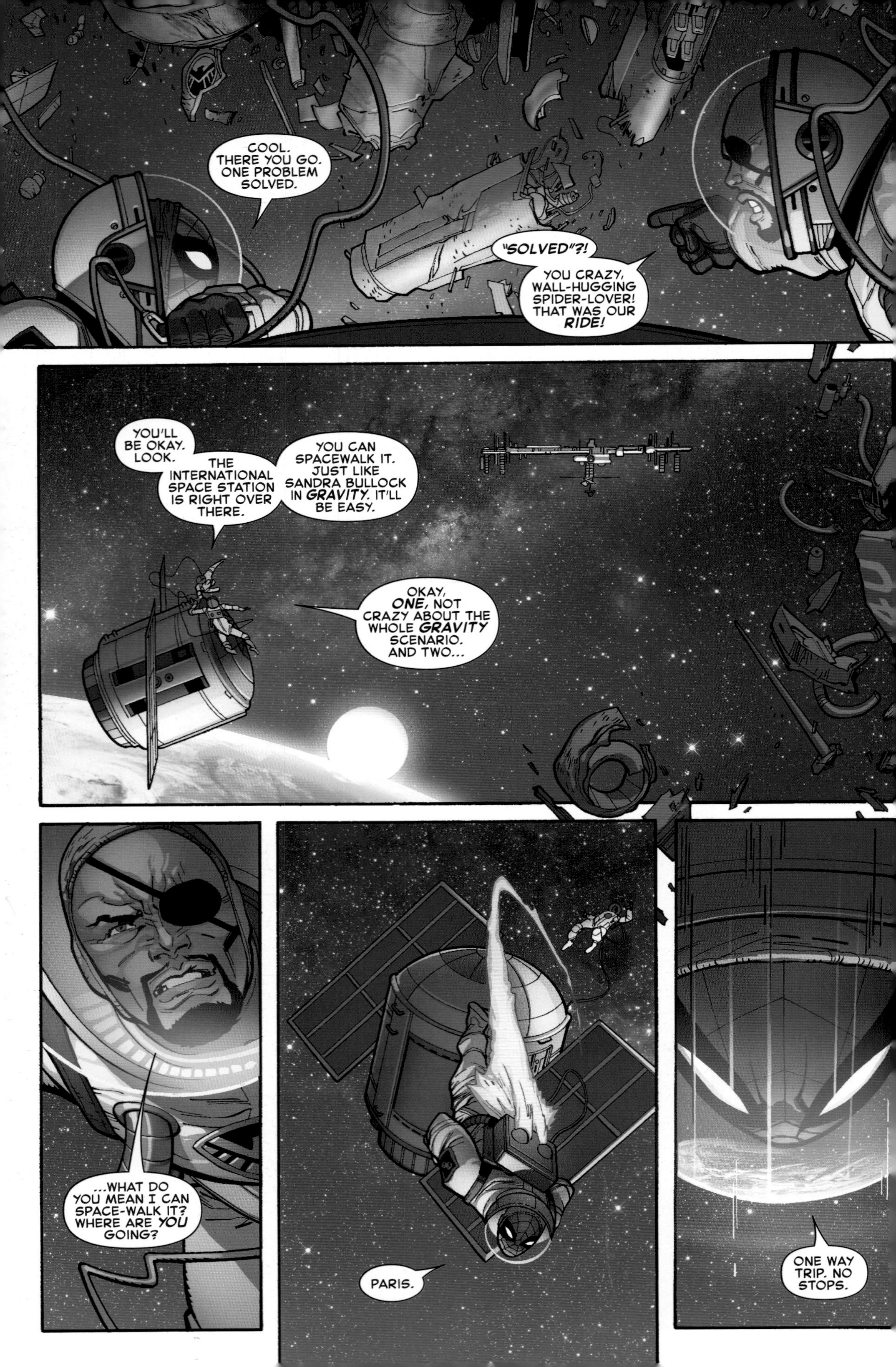
COOL. THERE YOU GO. ONE PROBLEM SOLVED.
"SOLVED"?!
YOU CRAZY, WALL-HUGGING SPIDER-LOVER! THAT WAS OUR RIDE!
YOU'LL BE OKAY. LOOK.
THE INTERNATIONAL SPACE STATION IS RIGHT OVER THERE.
YOU CAN SPACEWALK IT. JUST LIKE SANDRA BULLOCK IN GRAVITY. IT'LL BE EASY.
OKAY, ONE, NOT CRAZY ABOUT THE WHOLE GRAVITY SCENARIO. AND TWO...
...WHAT DO YOU MEAN I CAN SPACE-WALK IT? WHERE ARE YOU GOING?
PARIS.
ONE WAY TRIP. NO STOPS.

HE--HE LIVES.

HIS ROCKET'S DESTROYED, BUT--

--HE'S STILL COMING!

IMPOSSIBLE! THIS IS SPIDER-MAN WE'RE TALKING ABOUT. *NOT THOR!*

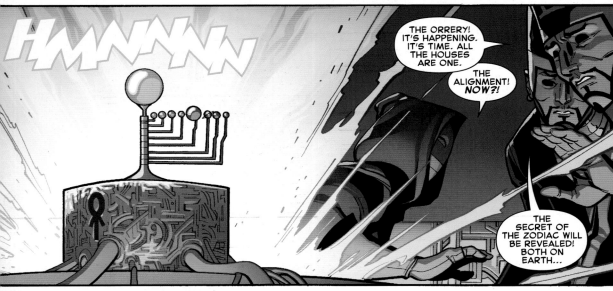

HMNNNNN

THE ORRERY! IT'S HAPPENING. IT'S TIME. ALL THE HOUSES ARE ONE.

THE ALIGNMENT! *NOW?!*

THE SECRET OF THE ZODIAC WILL BE REVEALED! BOTH ON EARTH...

...AND IN HEAVEN.

STOP THAT. YOU'RE CREEPING ME OUT.

THERE IS A NEW CONSTELLATION IN THE SKY! A *THIRTEENTH* SIGN!

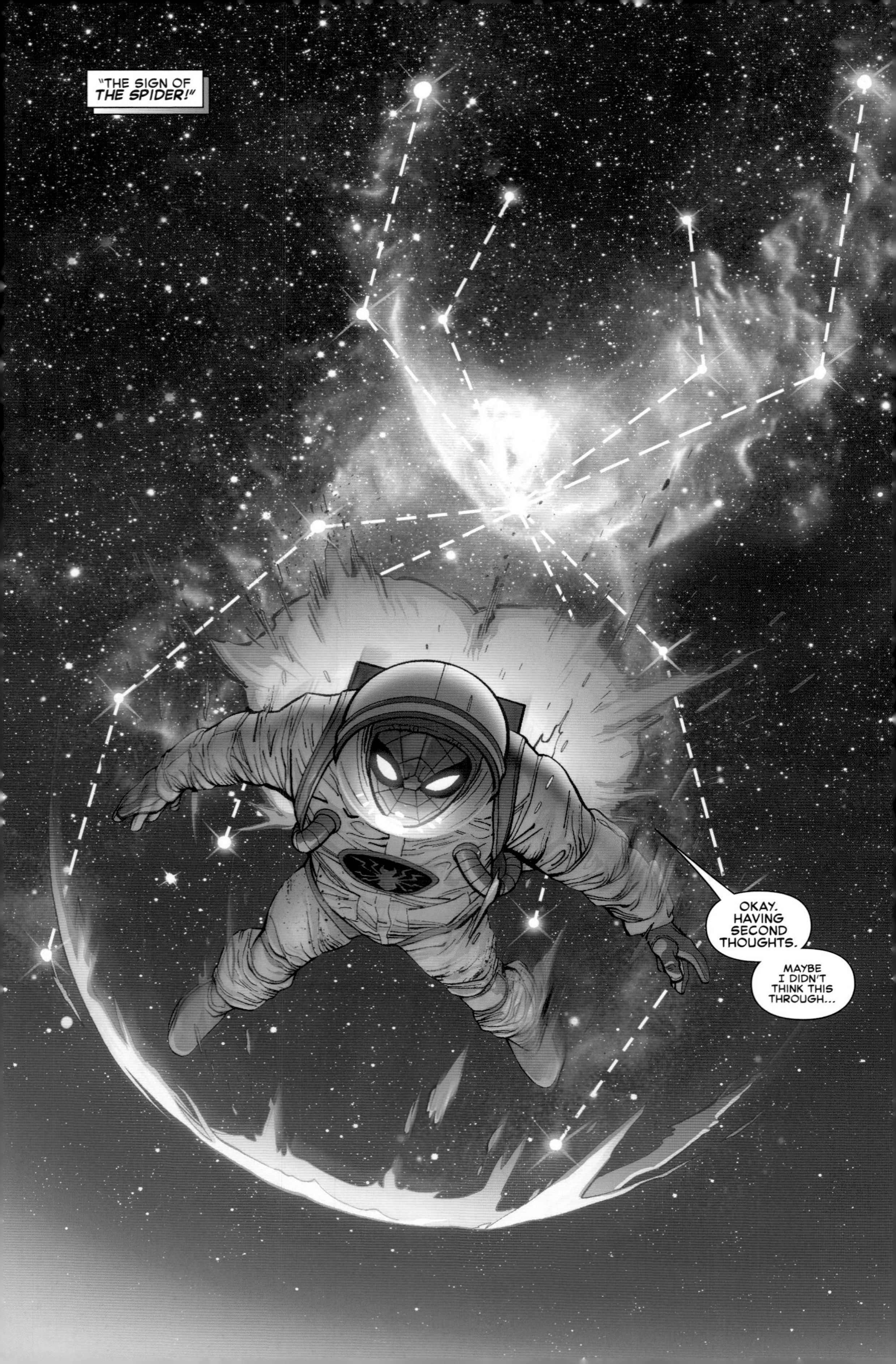
"THE SIGN OF THE SPIDER!"
OKAY. HAVING SECOND THOUGHTS.
MAYBE I DIDN'T THINK THIS THROUGH...

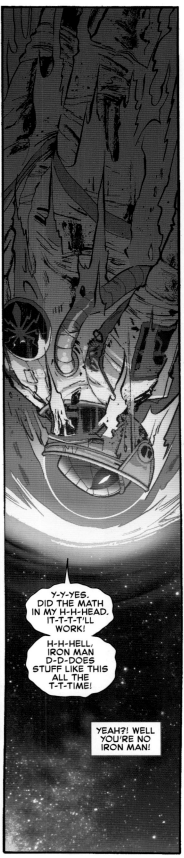

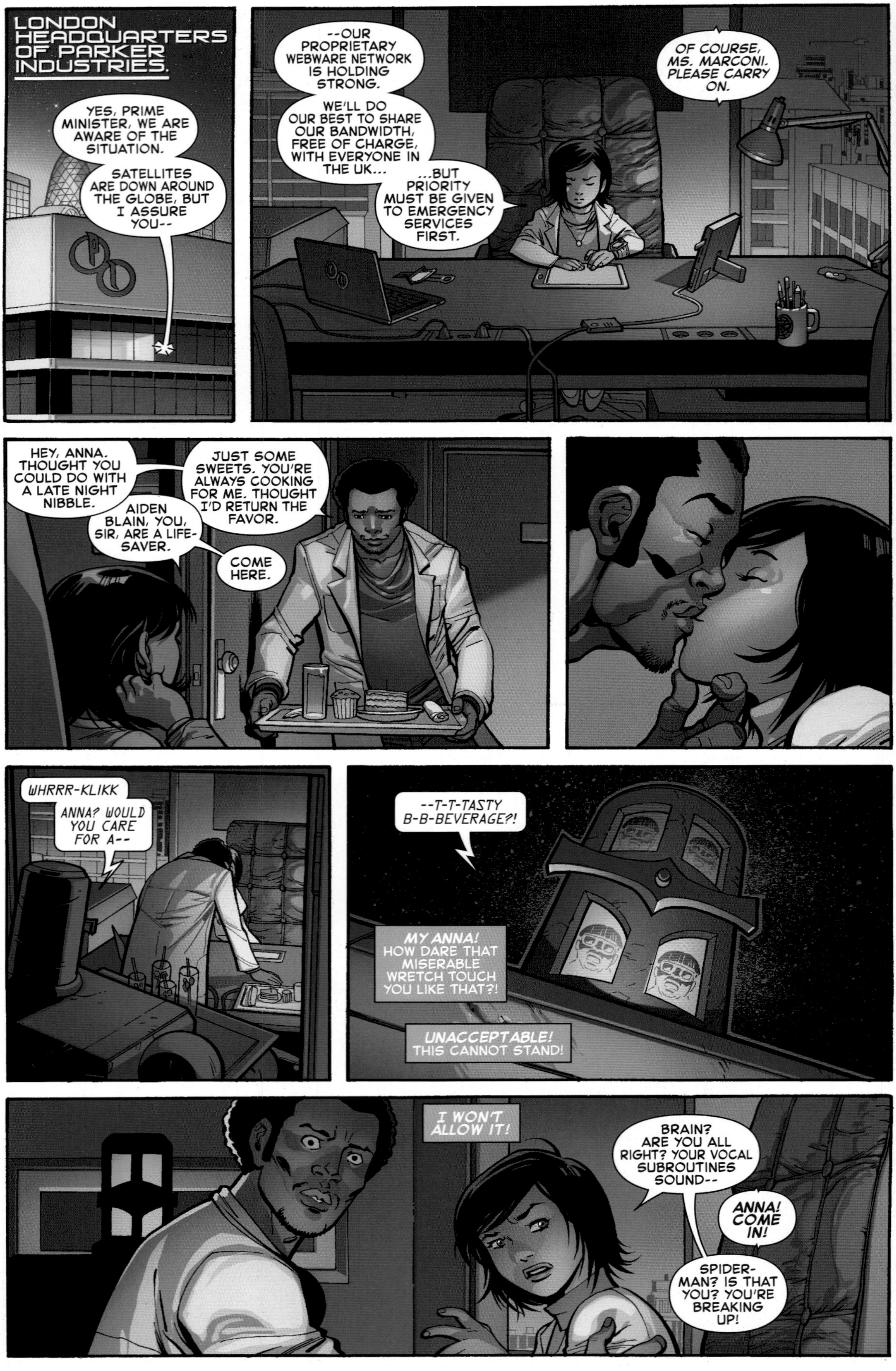
LONDON HEADQUARTERS OF PARKER INDUSTRIES.
YES, PRIME MINISTER, WE ARE AWARE OF THE SITUATION.
SATELLITES ARE DOWN AROUND THE GLOBE, BUT I ASSURE YOU--
--OUR PROPRIETARY WEBWARE NETWORK IS HOLDING STRONG.
WE'LL DO OUR BEST TO SHARE OUR BANDWIDTH, FREE OF CHARGE, WITH EVERYONE IN THE UK...
...BUT PRIORITY MUST BE GIVEN TO EMERGENCY SERVICES FIRST.
OF COURSE, MS. MARCONI. PLEASE CARRY ON.
HEY, ANNA. THOUGHT YOU COULD DO WITH A LATE NIGHT NIBBLE.
JUST SOME SWEETS. YOU'RE ALWAYS COOKING FOR ME. THOUGHT I'D RETURN THE FAVOR.
AIDEN BLAIN, YOU, SIR, ARE A LIFE-SAVER.
COME HERE.
WHRRR-KLIKK
ANNA? WOULD YOU CARE FOR A--
--T-T-TASTY B-B-BEVERAGE?!
MY ANNA! HOW DARE THAT MISERABLE WRETCH TOUCH YOU LIKE THAT?!
UNACCEPTABLE! THIS CANNOT STAND!
I WON'T ALLOW IT!
BRAIN? ARE YOU ALL RIGHT? YOUR VOCAL SUBROUTINES SOUND--
ANNA! COME IN!
SPIDER-MAN? IS THAT YOU? YOU'RE BREAKING UP!

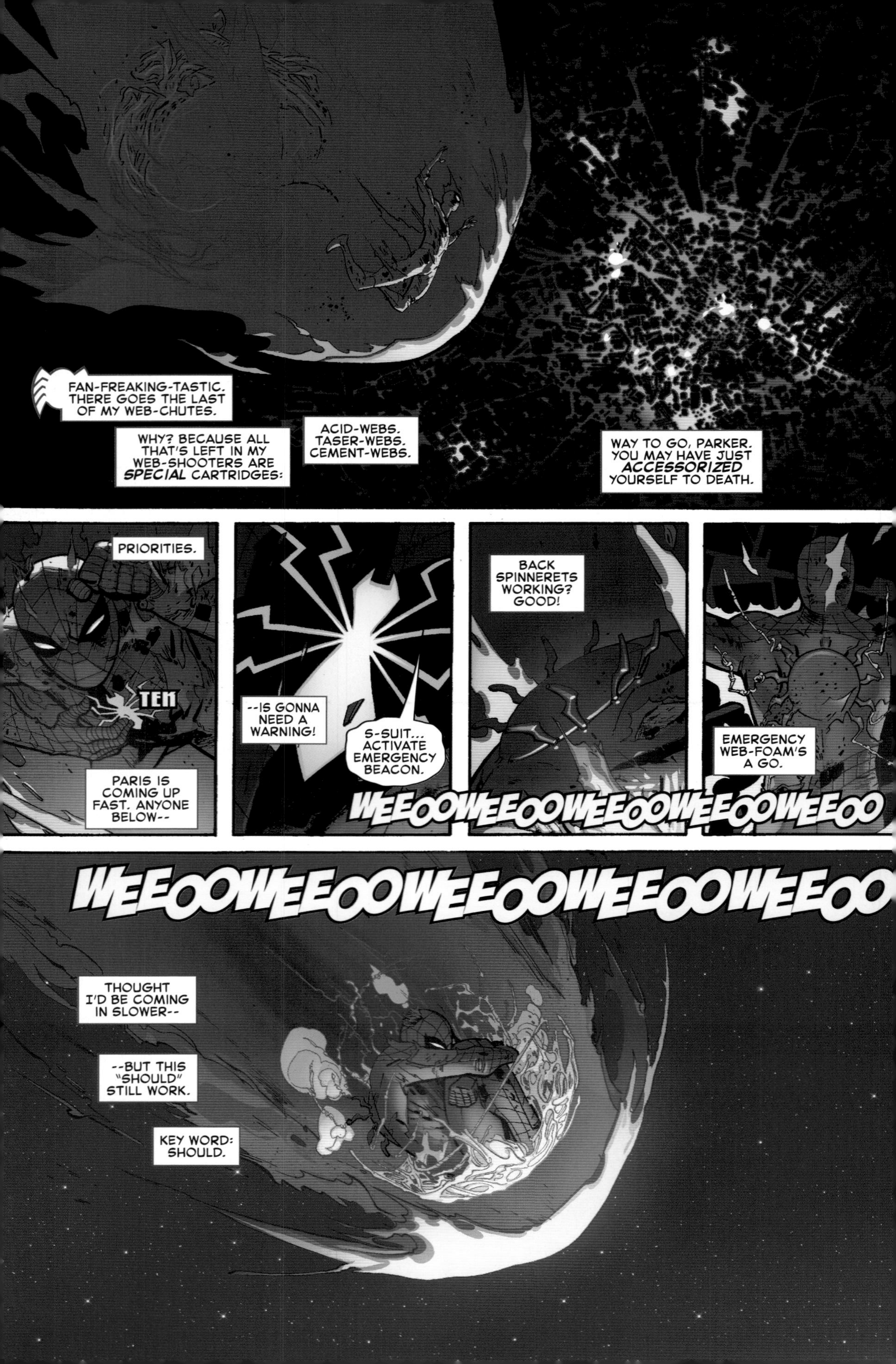

FAN-FREAKING-TASTIC. THERE GOES THE LAST OF MY WEB-CHUTES.
WHY? BECAUSE ALL THAT'S LEFT IN MY WEB-SHOOTERS ARE *SPECIAL* CARTRIDGES:
ACID-WEBS. TASER-WEBS. CEMENT-WEBS.
WAY TO GO, PARKER. YOU MAY HAVE JUST *ACCESSORIZED* YOURSELF TO DEATH.
PRIORITIES.
TEN
PARIS IS COMING UP FAST. ANYONE BELOW--
--IS GONNA NEED A WARNING!
S-SUIT... ACTIVATE EMERGENCY BEACON.
BACK SPINNERETS WORKING? GOOD!
EMERGENCY WEB-FOAM'S A GO.
WEEOOWEEOOWEEOOWEEOOWEEOO
WEEOOWEEOOWEEOOWEEOOWEEOO
THOUGHT I'D BE COMING IN SLOWER--
--BUT THIS "SHOULD" STILL WORK.
KEY WORD: SHOULD.

THIS IS GONNA HURT.
WEEOOWEEOOWEEOOWEEOOWEEOO
<WHAT IS THAT?>*
*TRANSLATED FROM FRENCH.
WEEOOWEEOOWEEOOWEEOOWEEOO
<A MISSILE!>
<MY GOD!>
<RUN!>
WEEOOWEEOOWEEOOWEEOOWEEOO
KAKROOM

OW.

YES! I'M ONE BIG BRUISE. SUIT'S A WRECK. BUT I *DID* IT!

SON OF A BISCUIT! FELL ALL THE WAY FROM *SPACE* AND SURVIVED!

EVERYONE OKAY OUT THERE? HANG ON, I'LL BE RIGHT--

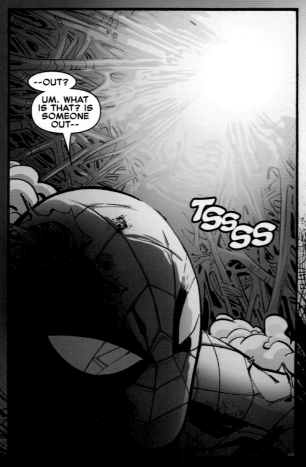

--OUT?

UM. WHAT IS THAT? IS SOMEONE OUT--

TSSSS

BWAKOOM

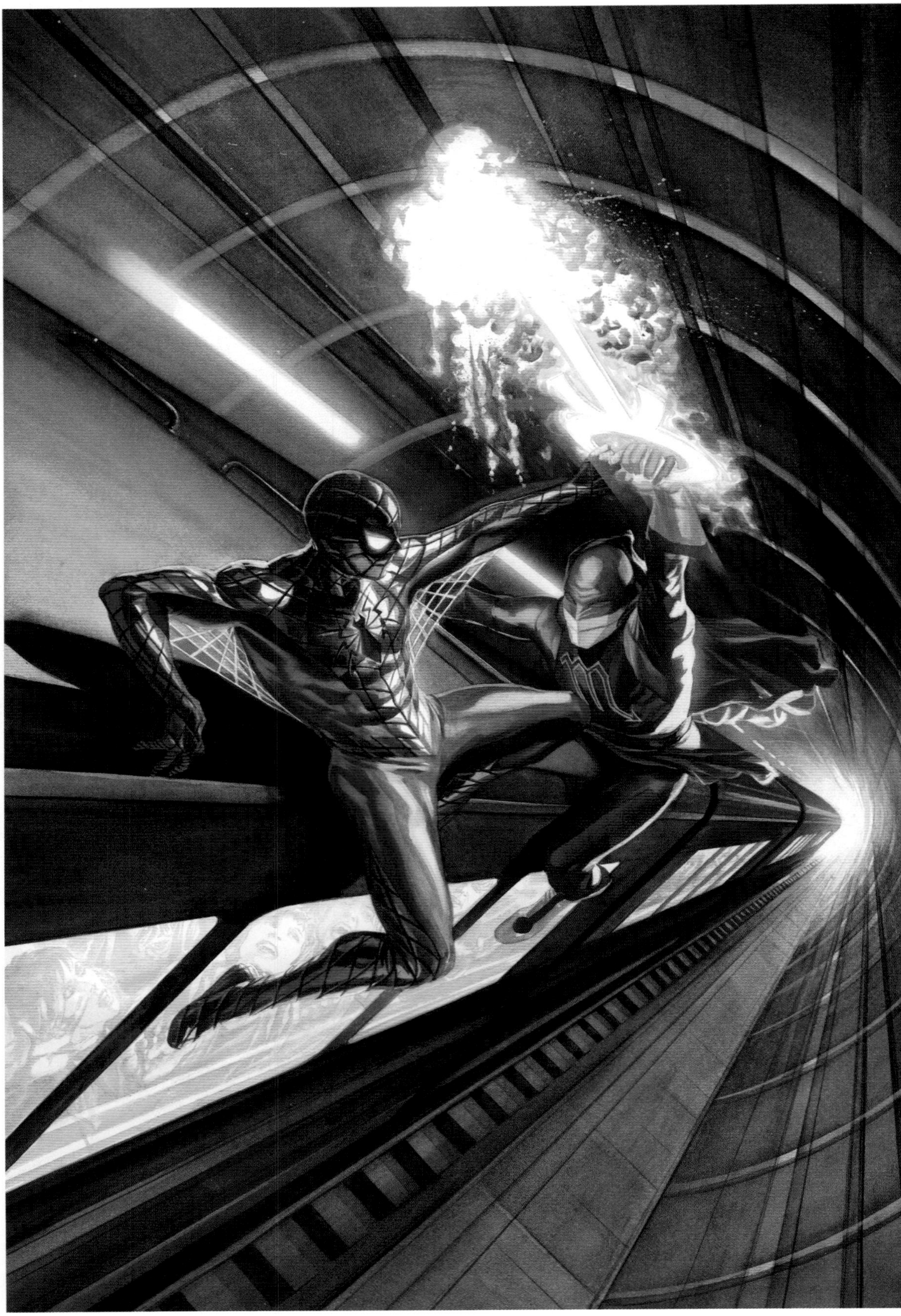

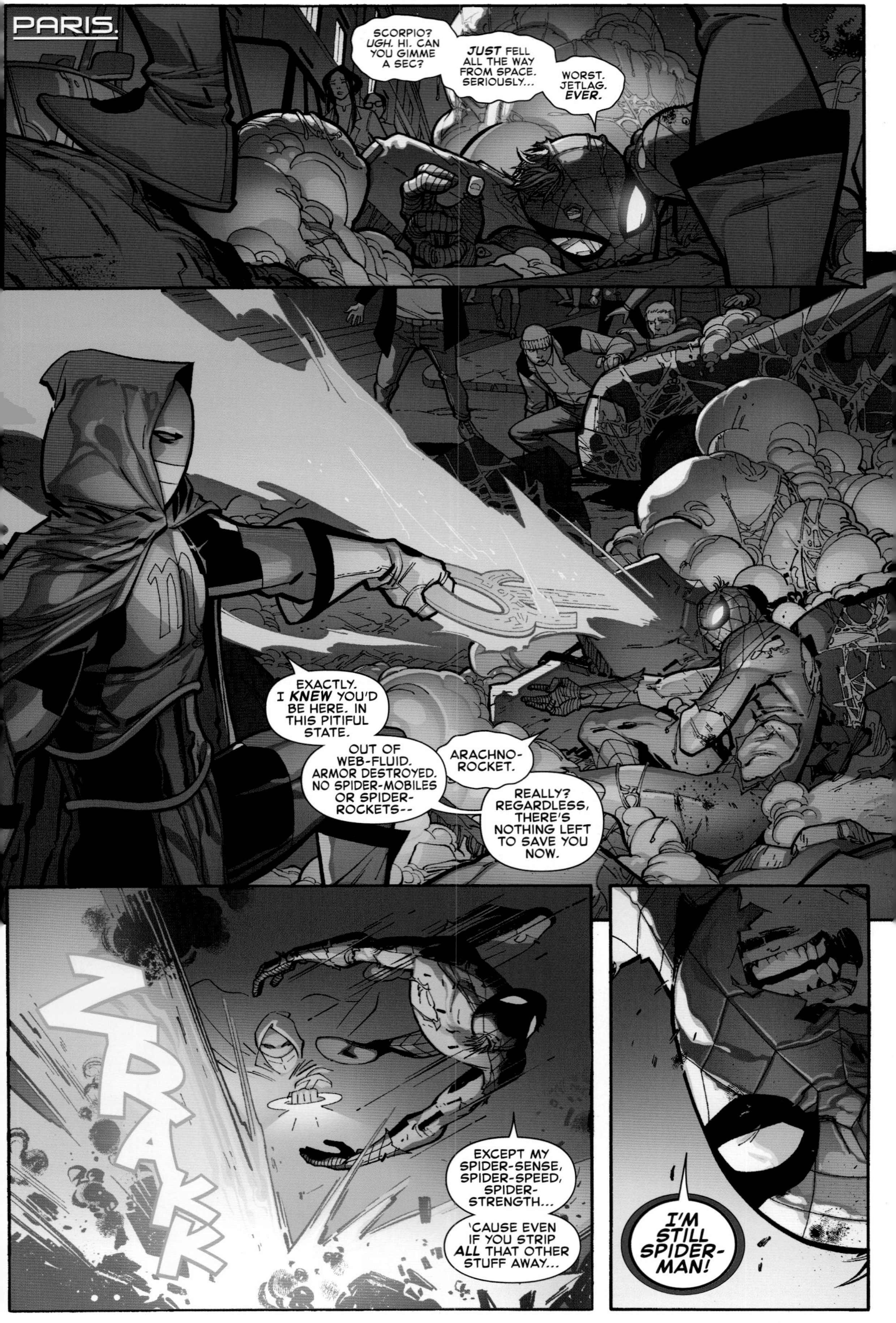
PARIS.
SCORPIO? UGH. HI. CAN YOU GIMME A SEC?
JUST FELL ALL THE WAY FROM SPACE. SERIOUSLY...
WORST. JETLAG. EVER.
EXACTLY. I KNEW YOU'D BE HERE. IN THIS PITIFUL STATE.
OUT OF WEB-FLUID. ARMOR DESTROYED. NO SPIDER-MOBILES OR SPIDER-ROCKETS--
ARACHNO-ROCKET.
REALLY? REGARDLESS, THERE'S NOTHING LEFT TO SAVE YOU NOW.
ZRAKK
EXCEPT MY SPIDER-SENSE, SPIDER-SPEED, SPIDER-STRENGTH...
'CAUSE EVEN IF YOU STRIP ALL THAT OTHER STUFF AWAY...
I'M STILL SPIDER-MAN!

AND I STILL HAVE MY *MOVES*.

HERE'S ONE A CERTAIN MASTER OF KUNG-FU TAUGHT ME!

TOO BAD IT'S USELESS AGAINST THE *ZODIAC KEY!*

THAT'S A NICE DOODAD YOU GOT THERE, SCORPY...

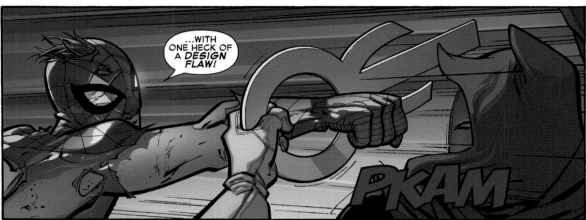

...WITH ONE HECK OF A *DESIGN FLAW!*

PKAM

UNFFF!

WELL PLAYED. BUT I KNOW *YOUR* FLAW, WALL-CRAWLER...

BYSTANDERS. YOU CARE MORE FOR OTHERS THAN YOUR *OWN* SKIN.

AH!

NO! CAN'T WEB THEM OUT OF THE WAY! USED UP ALL MY *NORMAL* WEBBING!

ALL THAT'S LEFT ARE *SPECIAL* CARTRIDGES.

ACID-WEBS! CONCRETE-WEBS! THAT'D KILL 'EM!

STOP WHAT YOU'RE DOING AND GET TO THE STATION *IMMEDIATELY.*

I HAVE THE PASSPORTS, TICKETS, AND EQUIPMENT. BUT WE MUST GO *NOW.*

BUT I CAN--

YOU *CAN'T.* PARISIANS ARE GETTING IN YOUR WAY, YES?

<BACK OFF! THIS MAN'S A HERO!">

<WANT HIM? YOU'LL HAVE TO GO THROUGH US! >

<WE STAND WITH SPIDER-MAN!>

THEY'RE NOTHING! ONE BLAST WOULD RIP RIGHT THROUGH THEM!

AND YOU'LL MISS THE TRAIN. AND THE ASCENSION. I'VE SEEN THAT FUTURE.

THERE'LL BE A MOTORCYCLE COMING ON YOUR LEFT. GRAB IT.

AND YOU'LL JUST MAKE IT IN TIME.

WOULD YOU RATHER WIN THE BATTLE OR THE WAR?

BUT I WAS *WINNING!*

I HATE YOU.

THOK

HEY!

YO. WHERE YA THINK *YOU'RE* GOIN'?

YEAH, YOU BETTER RUN!

PAFF

THERE. THAT SHOWED 'IM.

YAY ME...

YOU'VE STUDIED THE SCHEMATICS, ALEKSEI? YOU KNOW WHERE TO FIND THE MEN I WANT?

YEAH. THE LIZARD AND--

NOT THE LIZARD. *DR. CURT CONNORS.* I NEED HIS BRAIN. THE CLAWS, SCALES, AND TAIL ARE A PACKAGE DEAL.

BUT THE OTHER GUY ON THE LIST? I'VE WORKED WITH HIM BEFORE AND--

STOP TRYING TO THINK FOR ME.

THERE'S ONLY *ONE* WAY I NEED YOU TO USE *YOUR* HEAD, RHINO. UNDERSTOOD?

... YES.

GOOD...

"...NOW GO. DO THAT HEADBUTT-Y THING YOU DO SO WELL."

"MAKE DADDY PROUD."

KRA-KOOM

"YOU HAVE REACHED YOUR DESTINATION. WHIRR-CLICK-ICK..."

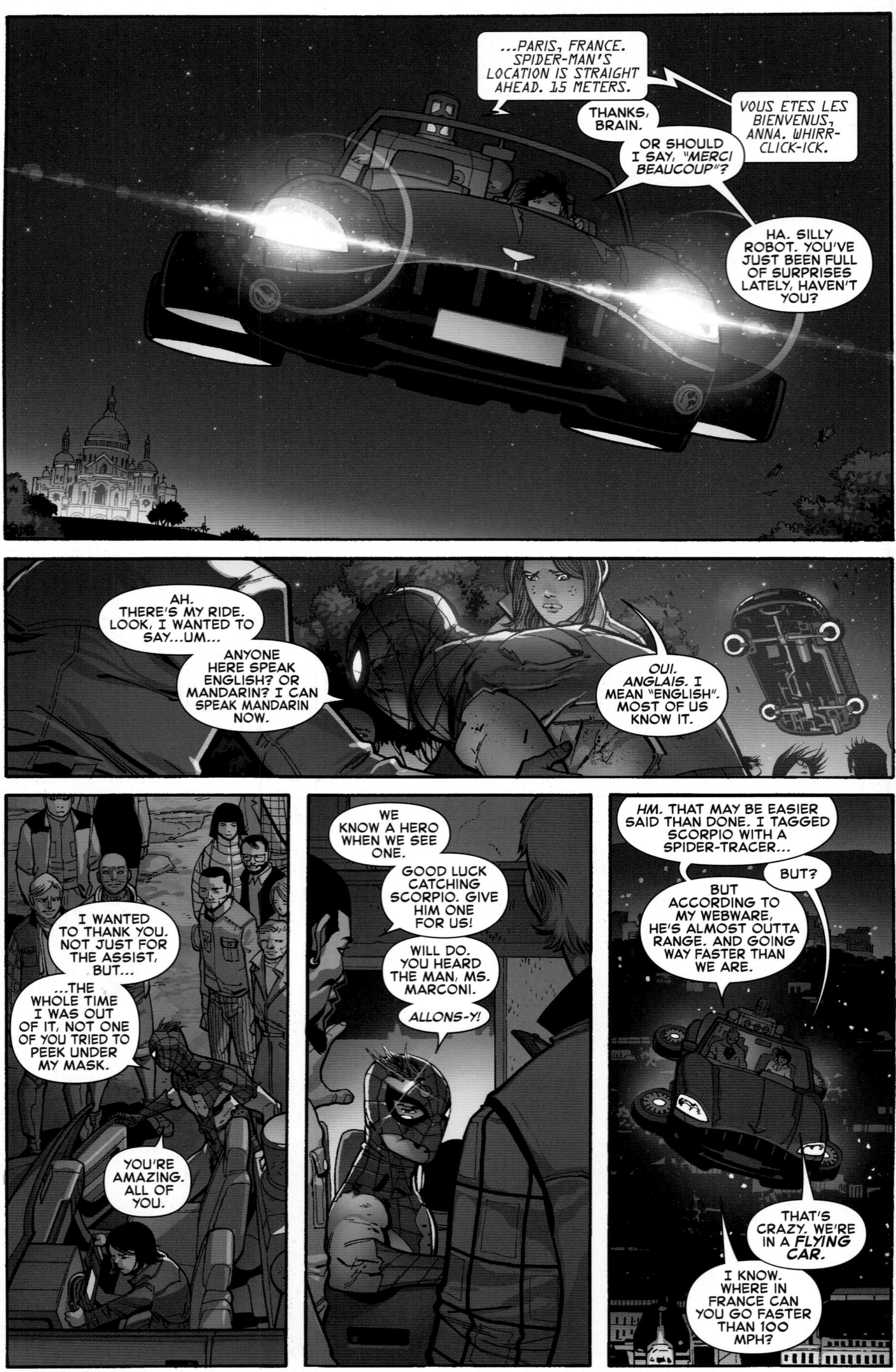
...PARIS, FRANCE. SPIDER-MAN'S LOCATION IS STRAIGHT AHEAD. 15 METERS.
THANKS, BRAIN.
OR SHOULD I SAY, "MERCI BEAUCOUP"?
VOUS ETES LES BIENVENUS, ANNA. WHIRR-CLICK-ICK.
HA. SILLY ROBOT. YOU'VE JUST BEEN FULL OF SURPRISES LATELY, HAVEN'T YOU?
AH. THERE'S MY RIDE. LOOK, I WANTED TO SAY...UM...
ANYONE HERE SPEAK ENGLISH? OR MANDARIN? I CAN SPEAK MANDARIN NOW.
OUI. ANGLAIS. I MEAN "ENGLISH". MOST OF US KNOW IT.
I WANTED TO THANK YOU. NOT JUST FOR THE ASSIST, BUT...
...THE WHOLE TIME I WAS OUT OF IT, NOT ONE OF YOU TRIED TO PEEK UNDER MY MASK.
YOU'RE AMAZING. ALL OF YOU.
WE KNOW A HERO WHEN WE SEE ONE.
GOOD LUCK CATCHING SCORPIO. GIVE HIM ONE FOR US!
WILL DO. YOU HEARD THE MAN, MS. MARCONI.
ALLONS-Y!
HM. THAT MAY BE EASIER SAID THAN DONE. I TAGGED SCORPIO WITH A SPIDER-TRACER...
BUT?
BUT ACCORDING TO MY WEBWARE, HE'S ALMOST OUTTA RANGE. AND GOING WAY FASTER THAN WE ARE.
THAT'S CRAZY. WE'RE IN A FLYING CAR.
I KNOW. WHERE IN FRANCE CAN YOU GO FASTER THAN 100 MPH?

THE CHUNNEL!

I'M PUNCHING IT!

ALL RIGHT! WE MIGHT JUST PULL THIS OFF.

I STILL DON'T KNOW WHERE SCORPIO'S GOING...

...BUT IF IT WAS *MORE* IMPORTANT THAN FINISHING ME OFF, THAT CAN'T BE GOOD.

SAY, DID YOU REMEMBER TO BRING--

YOUR SPARE SUIT AND MORE WEB-FLUID... DOC-TOR PARKER. WHIRR-CLICK.

THANKS, BRAIN. BUT IT'S "SPIDER-MAN" WHEN I'M IN THE MASK, OKAY?

WHILE I'VE GOT YOU, CAN YOU DO A QUICK MEDICAL SCAN?

I'M SO BASHED UP, I DON'T KNOW WHAT'S OUT OF PLACE.

WHIRR-CLICK-ICK. YOUR BODY WAS-- IS--PERFECT.

QUICK TO HEAL. POWERFUL. THE ULTIMATE VESSEL.

WHOA. THAT WAS...ODD. NOW I'M FEELING SELF-CONSCIOUS AND HALF-DRESSED.

WHAT ROAD? ALSO, AIN'T NOTHING I HAVEN'T SEEN BEFORE, PETE.

ANNA MARIA MARCONI! EYES ON THE ROAD.

GUYS, FOCUS. WE GOT A TRAIN TO CATCH.

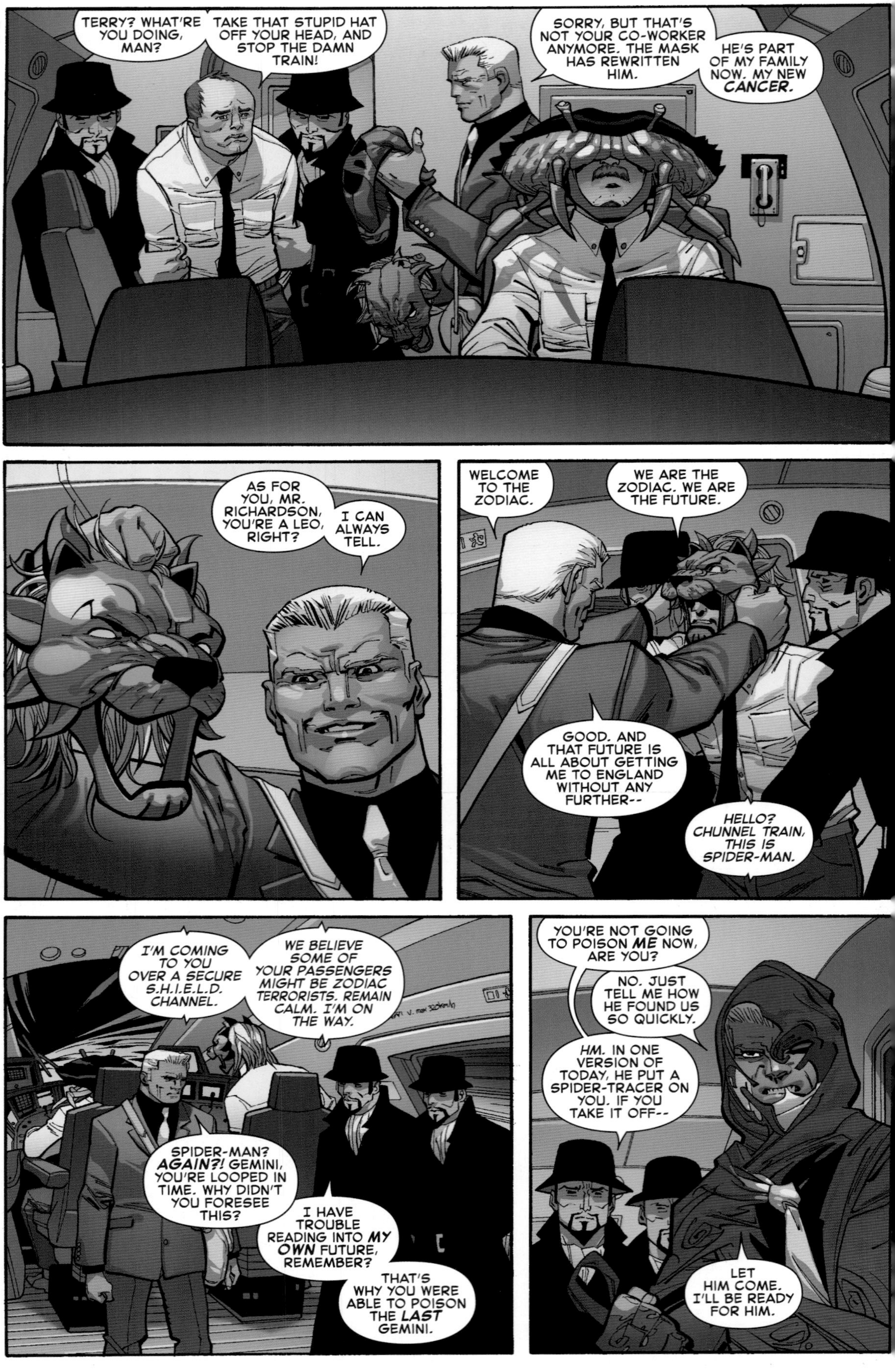
TERRY? WHAT'RE YOU DOING, MAN?
TAKE THAT STUPID HAT OFF YOUR HEAD, AND STOP THE DAMN TRAIN!
SORRY, BUT THAT'S NOT YOUR CO-WORKER ANYMORE. THE MASK HAS REWRITTEN HIM.
HE'S PART OF MY FAMILY NOW. MY NEW CANCER.
AS FOR YOU, MR. RICHARDSON, YOU'RE A LEO, RIGHT?
I CAN ALWAYS TELL.
WELCOME TO THE ZODIAC.
WE ARE THE ZODIAC. WE ARE THE FUTURE.
GOOD. AND THAT FUTURE IS ALL ABOUT GETTING ME TO ENGLAND WITHOUT ANY FURTHER--
HELLO? CHUNNEL TRAIN, THIS IS SPIDER-MAN.
I'M COMING TO YOU OVER A SECURE S.H.I.E.L.D. CHANNEL.
WE BELIEVE SOME OF YOUR PASSENGERS MIGHT BE ZODIAC TERRORISTS. REMAIN CALM. I'M ON THE WAY.
SPIDER-MAN? AGAIN?! GEMINI, YOU'RE LOOPED IN TIME. WHY DIDN'T YOU FORESEE THIS?
I HAVE TROUBLE READING INTO MY OWN FUTURE, REMEMBER?
THAT'S WHY YOU WERE ABLE TO POISON THE LAST GEMINI.
YOU'RE NOT GOING TO POISON ME NOW, ARE YOU?
NO. JUST TELL ME HOW HE FOUND US SO QUICKLY.
HM. IN ONE VERSION OF TODAY, HE PUT A SPIDER-TRACER ON YOU. IF YOU TAKE IT OFF--
LET HIM COME. I'LL BE READY FOR HIM.

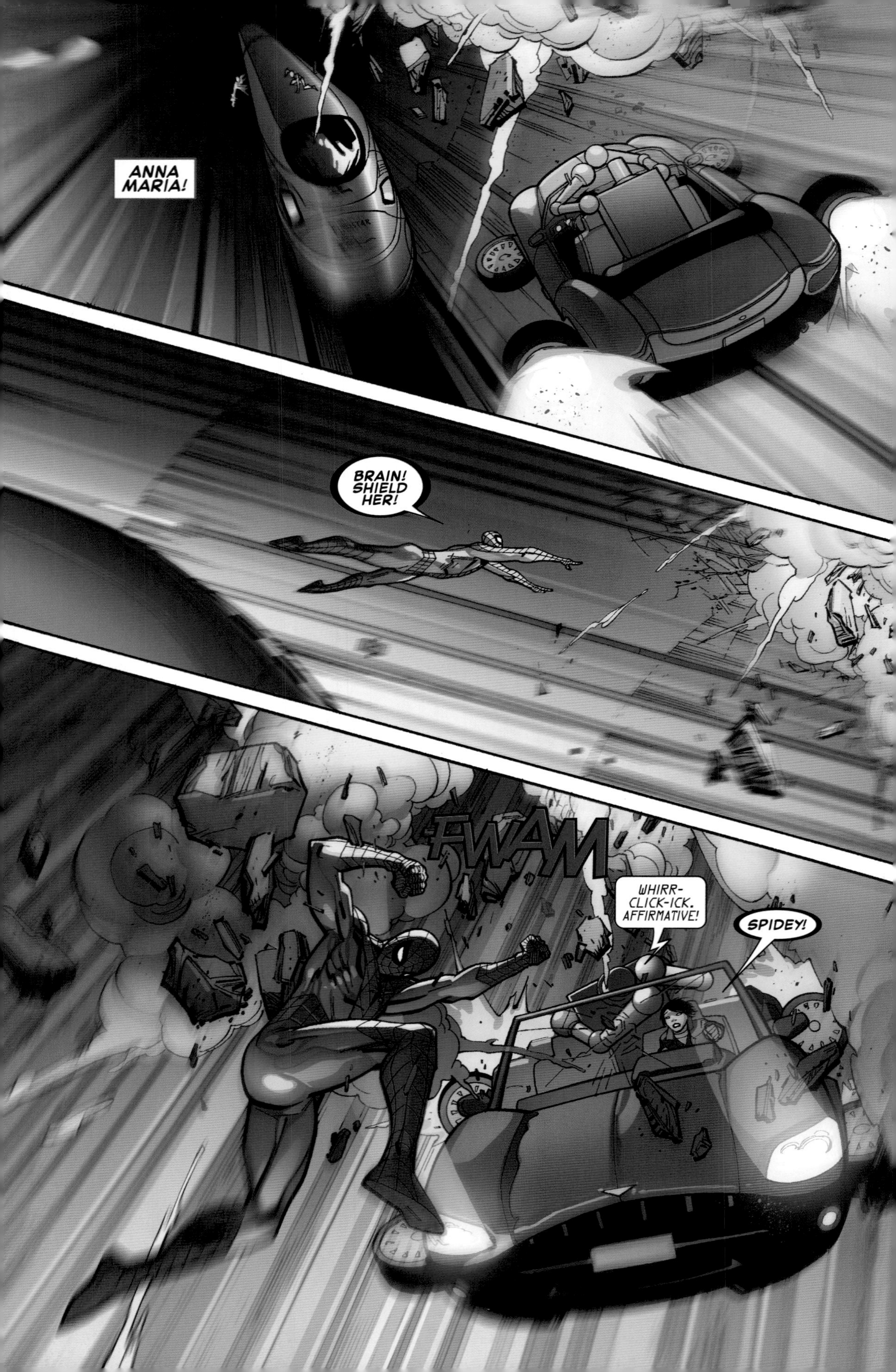
ANNA MARIA!
BRAIN! SHIELD HER!
FWAM
WHIRR-CLICK-ICK. AFFIRMATIVE!
SPIDEY!

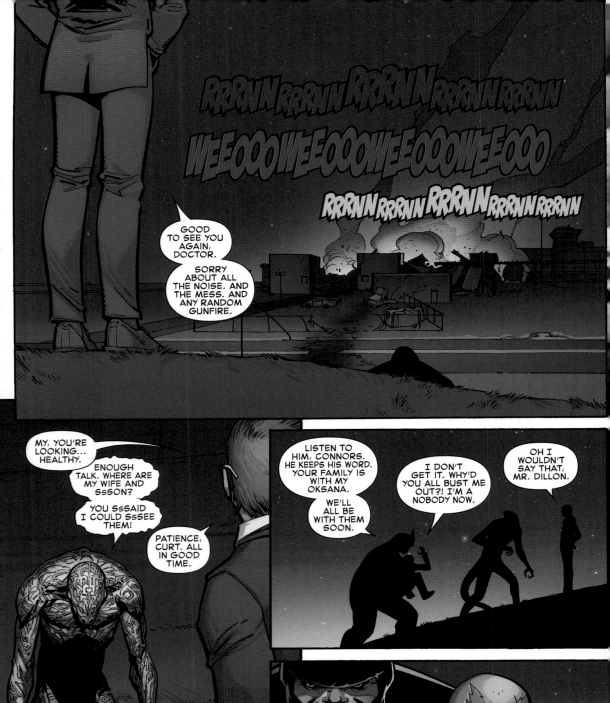

RRRNN RRRNN RRRNN RRRNN RRRNN

WEEOOOWEEOOOWEEOOOWEEOOO

RRRNN RRRNN RRRNN RRRNN RRRNN

GOOD TO SEE YOU AGAIN, DOCTOR.

SORRY ABOUT ALL THE NOISE. AND THE MESS. AND ANY RANDOM GUNFIRE.

MY, YOU'RE LOOKING... HEALTHY.

ENOUGH TALK. WHERE ARE MY WIFE AND SssSON?

YOU SssSAID I COULD SssSEE THEM!

PATIENCE, CURT. ALL IN GOOD TIME.

LISTEN TO HIM, CONNORS. HE KEEPS HIS WORD. YOUR FAMILY IS WITH MY OKSANA.

WE'LL ALL BE WITH THEM SOON.

I DON'T GET IT. WHY'D YOU ALL BUST ME OUT?! I'M A NOBODY NOW.

OH I WOULDN'T SAY THAT, MR. DILLON.

BUT THAT'S IT, I'M JUST MAX DILLON. I AIN'T ELECTRO NO MORE.

THERE AIN'T NOTHING I CAN DO FOR YA.

TRUST ME, MAX. I'M THE MAN WHO CAN MAKE MIRACLES.

THE REAL QUESTION IS: WHAT CAN I DO FOR YOU?

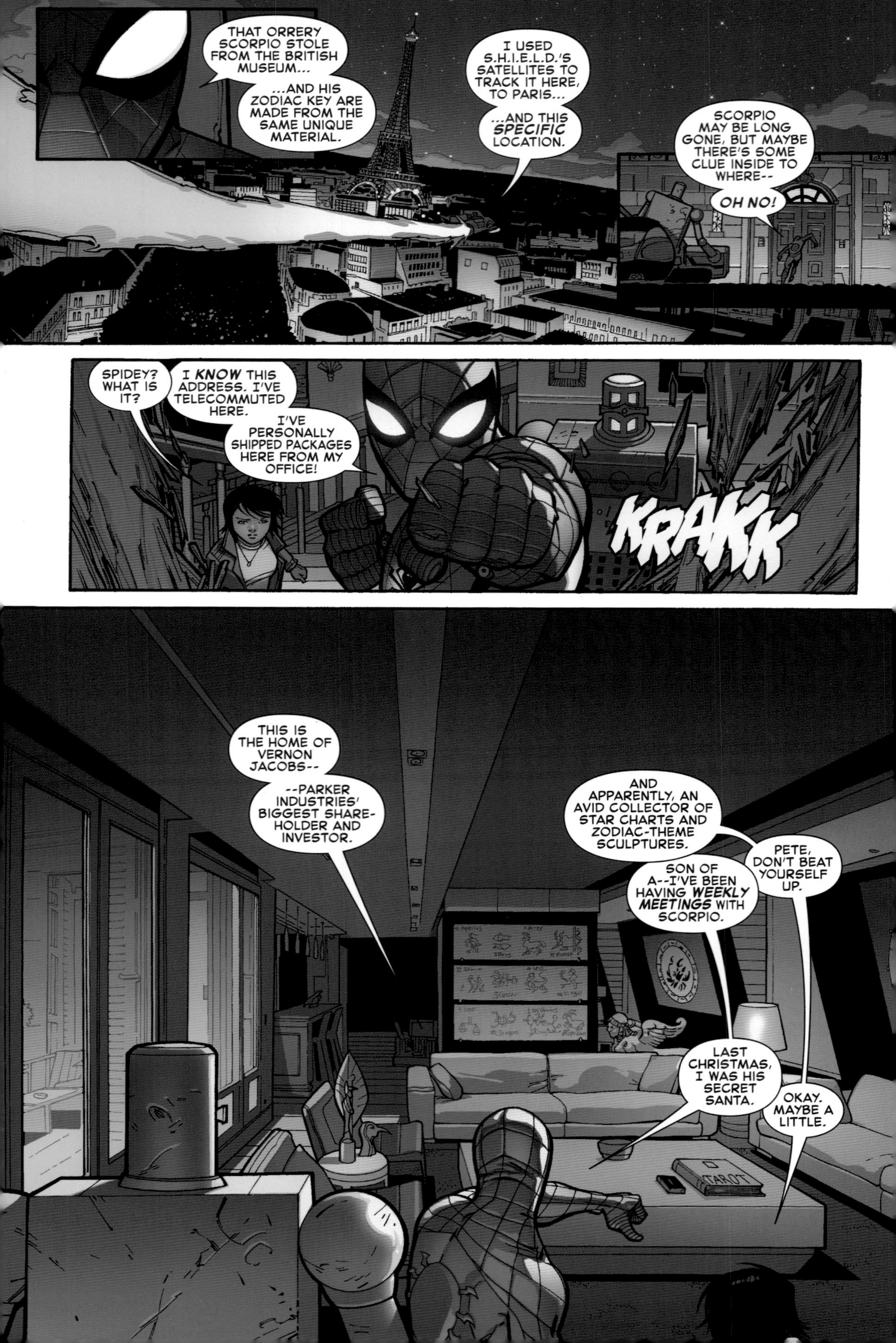
THAT ORRERY SCORPIO STOLE FROM THE BRITISH MUSEUM...
...AND HIS ZODIAC KEY ARE MADE FROM THE SAME UNIQUE MATERIAL.
I USED S.H.I.E.L.D.'S SATELLITES TO TRACK IT HERE, TO PARIS...
...AND THIS SPECIFIC LOCATION.
SCORPIO MAY BE LONG GONE, BUT MAYBE THERE'S SOME CLUE INSIDE TO WHERE--
OH NO!
SPIDEY? WHAT IS IT?
I KNOW THIS ADDRESS. I'VE TELECOMMUTED HERE.
I'VE PERSONALLY SHIPPED PACKAGES HERE FROM MY OFFICE!
KRAKK
THIS IS THE HOME OF VERNON JACOBS--
--PARKER INDUSTRIES' BIGGEST SHARE-HOLDER AND INVESTOR.
AND APPARENTLY, AN AVID COLLECTOR OF STAR CHARTS AND ZODIAC-THEME SCULPTURES.
SON OF A--I'VE BEEN HAVING WEEKLY MEETINGS WITH SCORPIO.
PETE, DON'T BEAT YOURSELF UP.
LAST CHRISTMAS, I WAS HIS SECRET SANTA.
OKAY. MAYBE A LITTLE.
TAROT

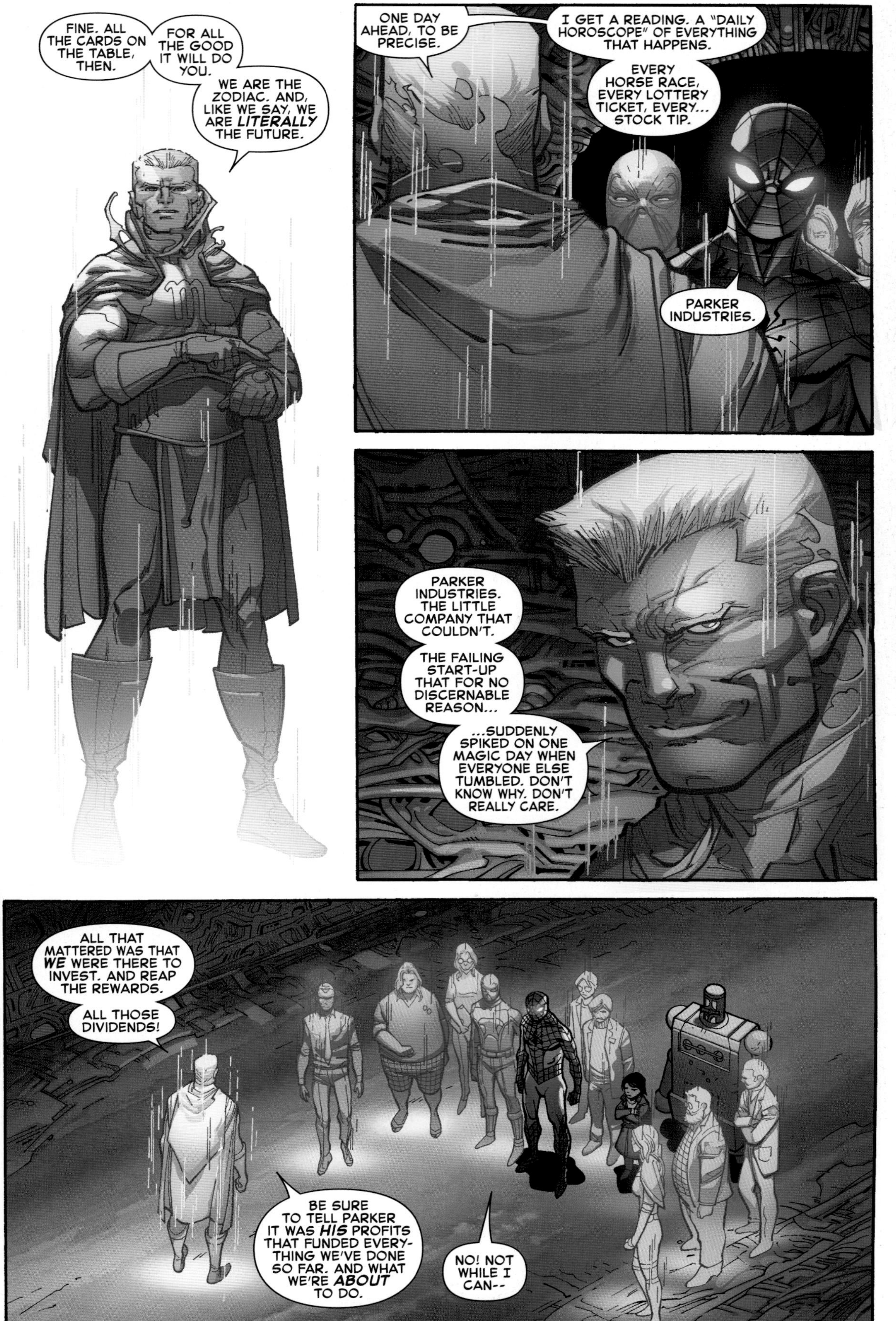
FINE. ALL THE CARDS ON THE TABLE, THEN.
FOR ALL THE GOOD IT WILL DO YOU.
WE ARE THE ZODIAC. AND, LIKE WE SAY, WE ARE *LITERALLY* THE FUTURE.
ONE DAY AHEAD, TO BE PRECISE.
I GET A READING. A "DAILY HOROSCOPE" OF EVERYTHING THAT HAPPENS.
EVERY HORSE RACE, EVERY LOTTERY TICKET, EVERY... STOCK TIP.
PARKER INDUSTRIES.
PARKER INDUSTRIES. THE LITTLE COMPANY THAT COULDN'T.
THE FAILING START-UP THAT FOR NO DISCERNABLE REASON...
...SUDDENLY SPIKED ON ONE MAGIC DAY WHEN EVERYONE ELSE TUMBLED. DON'T KNOW WHY. DON'T REALLY CARE.
ALL THAT MATTERED WAS THAT *WE* WERE THERE TO INVEST. AND REAP THE REWARDS.
ALL THOSE DIVIDENDS!
BE SURE TO TELL PARKER IT WAS *HIS* PROFITS THAT FUNDED EVERY-THING WE'VE DONE SO FAR. AND WHAT WE'RE *ABOUT* TO DO.
NO! NOT WHILE I CAN--

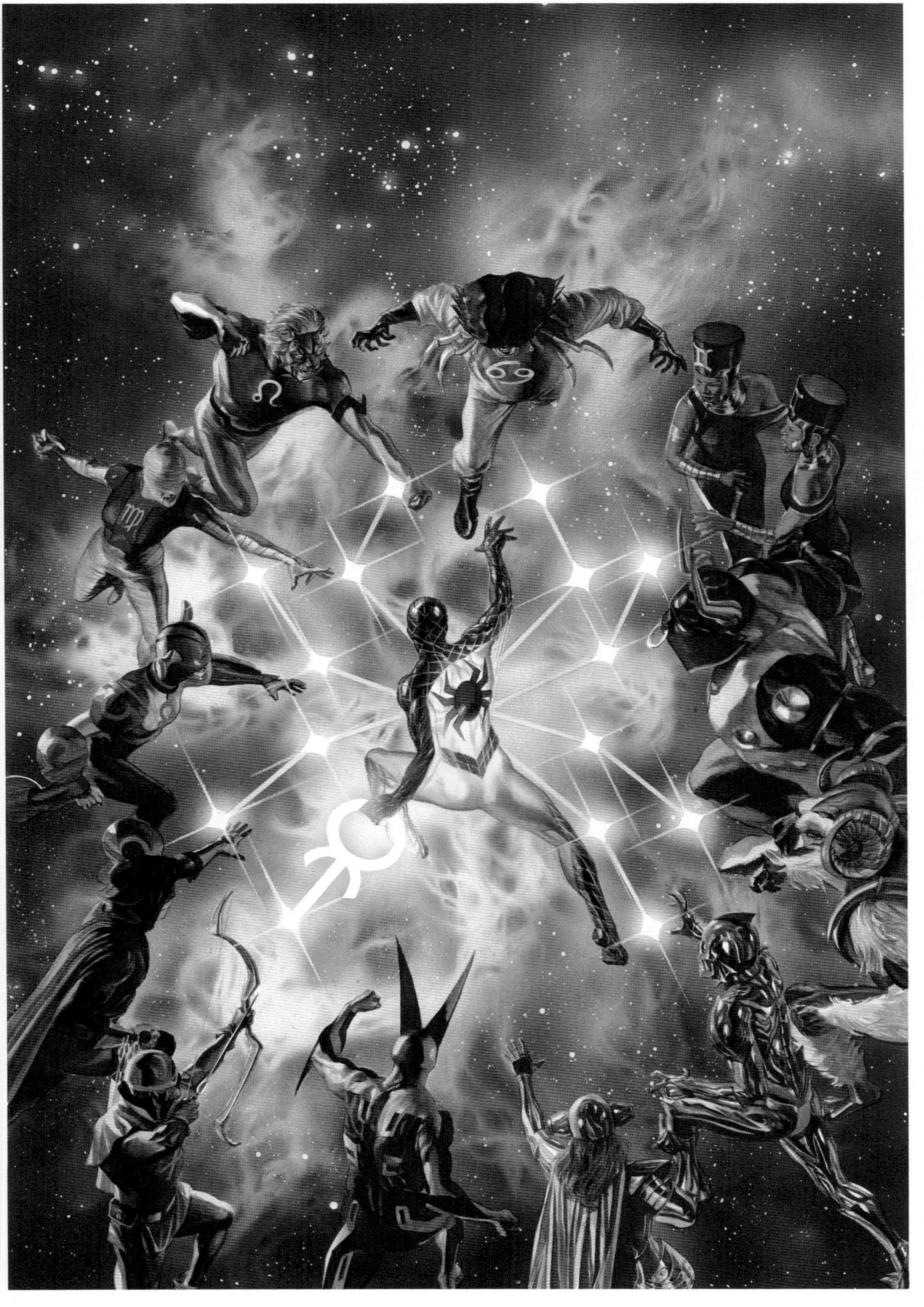

BLAZE A TRAIL! SHOW ME!

THE DOORWAY.

AT LAST, IT IS REVEALED.

MIDNIGHT. THE DAY IS OVER.

A NEW DAY BEGINS.

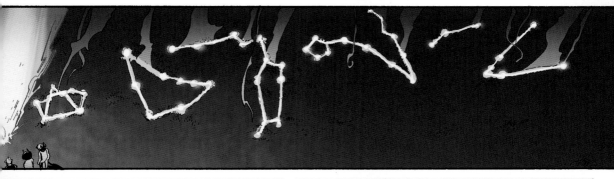

...I HAVE TO LOOP IN TIME AGAIN.

OR I CAN'T TELL YOU WHAT WILL HAPPEN ONE DAY INTO--

IT'S GONE. I DON'T KNOW WHAT'S NEXT.

WHO CARES?

BUT WHAT IF SPIDER-MAN INTERFERES AGAIN?

HERE! I'LL SAVE YOU THE TROUBLE!

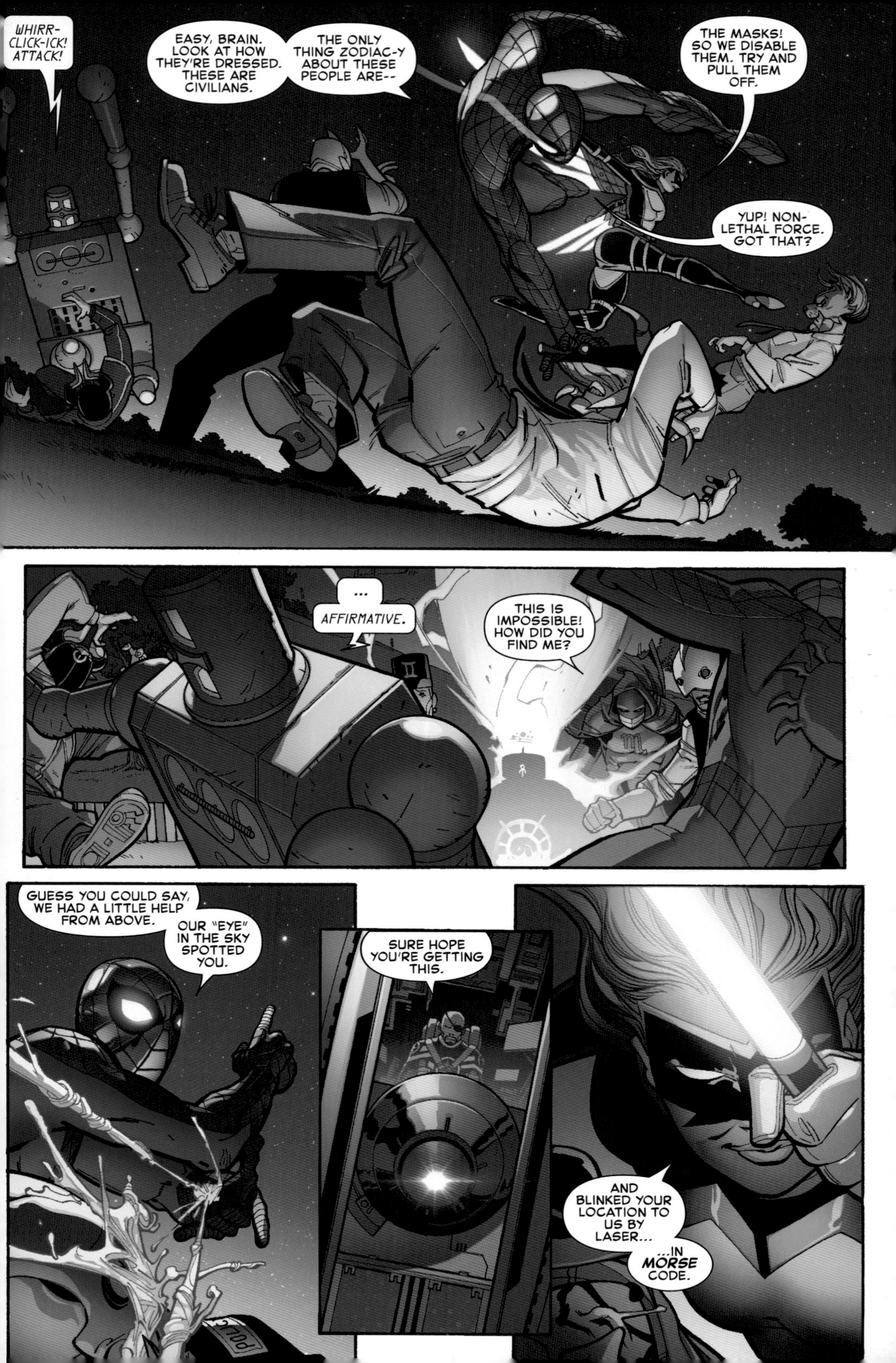
WHIRR-CLICK-ICK! ATTACK!
EASY, BRAIN. LOOK AT HOW THEY'RE DRESSED. THESE ARE CIVILIANS.
THE ONLY THING ZODIAC-Y ABOUT THESE PEOPLE ARE--
THE MASKS! SO WE DISABLE THEM. TRY AND PULL THEM OFF.
YUP! NON-LETHAL FORCE. GOT THAT?
... AFFIRMATIVE.
THIS IS IMPOSSIBLE! HOW DID YOU FIND ME?
GUESS YOU COULD SAY, WE HAD A LITTLE HELP FROM ABOVE.
OUR "EYE" IN THE SKY SPOTTED YOU.
SURE HOPE YOU'RE GETTING THIS.
AND BLINKED YOUR LOCATION TO US BY LASER...
...IN MORSE CODE.

ALL DOWN. BOTH FRIEND AND FOE. IT DOESN'T MATTER.

RRUNKKGH

THIS WAS NEVER ABOUT THE ZODIAC...

...JUST ME.

AND NO ONE ELSE.

KLIK

UGH...

C'MON, PARKER...

...GET UP. YOU CAN DO THIS...

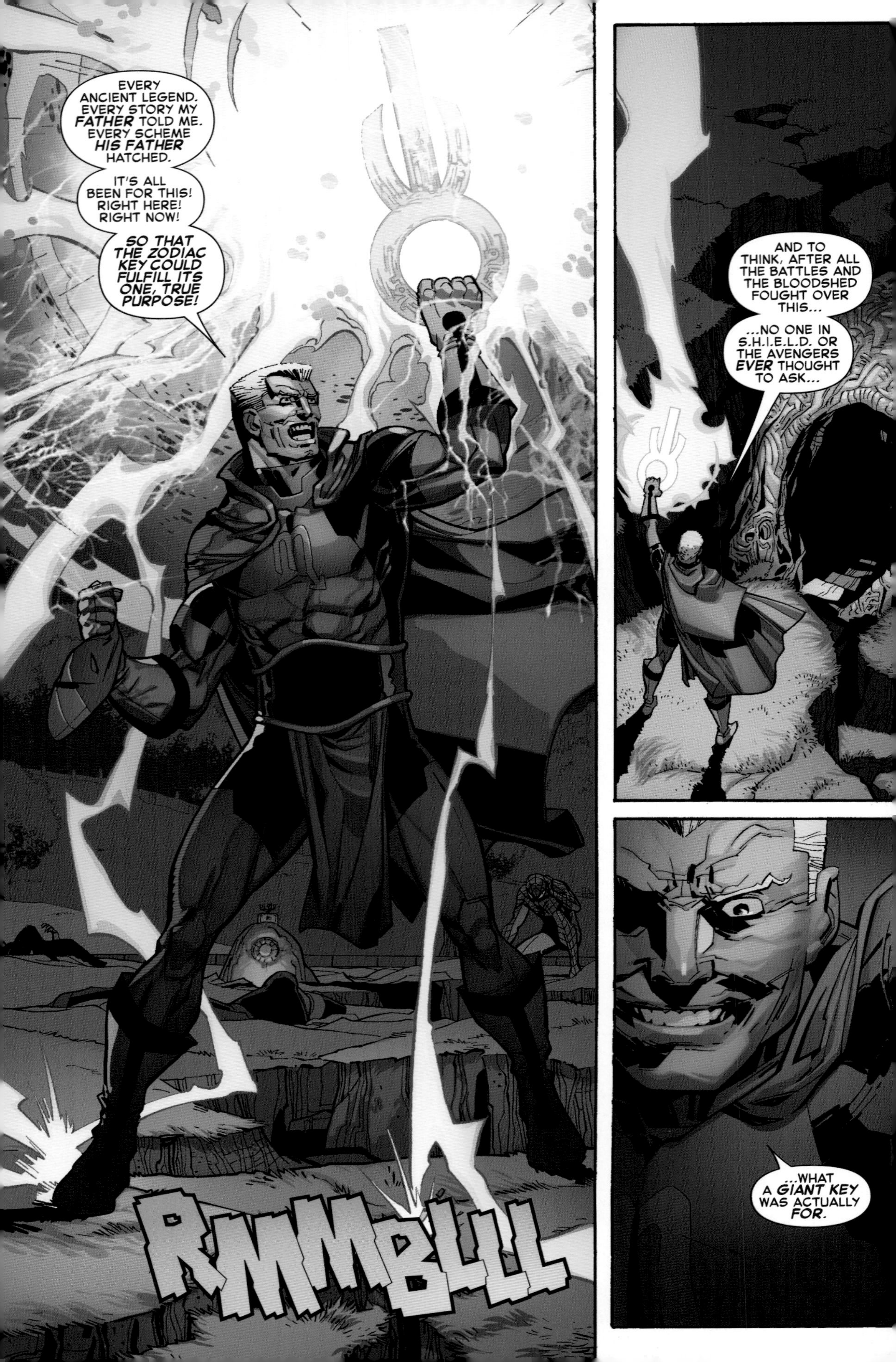
EVERY ANCIENT LEGEND. EVERY STORY MY FATHER TOLD ME. EVERY SCHEME HIS FATHER HATCHED.
IT'S ALL BEEN FOR THIS! RIGHT HERE! RIGHT NOW!
SO THAT THE ZODIAC KEY COULD FULFILL ITS ONE, TRUE PURPOSE!
RMMBLLL
AND TO THINK, AFTER ALL THE BATTLES AND THE BLOODSHED FOUGHT OVER THIS...
...NO ONE IN S.H.I.E.L.D. OR THE AVENGERS EVER THOUGHT TO ASK...
...WHAT A GIANT KEY WAS ACTUALLY FOR.

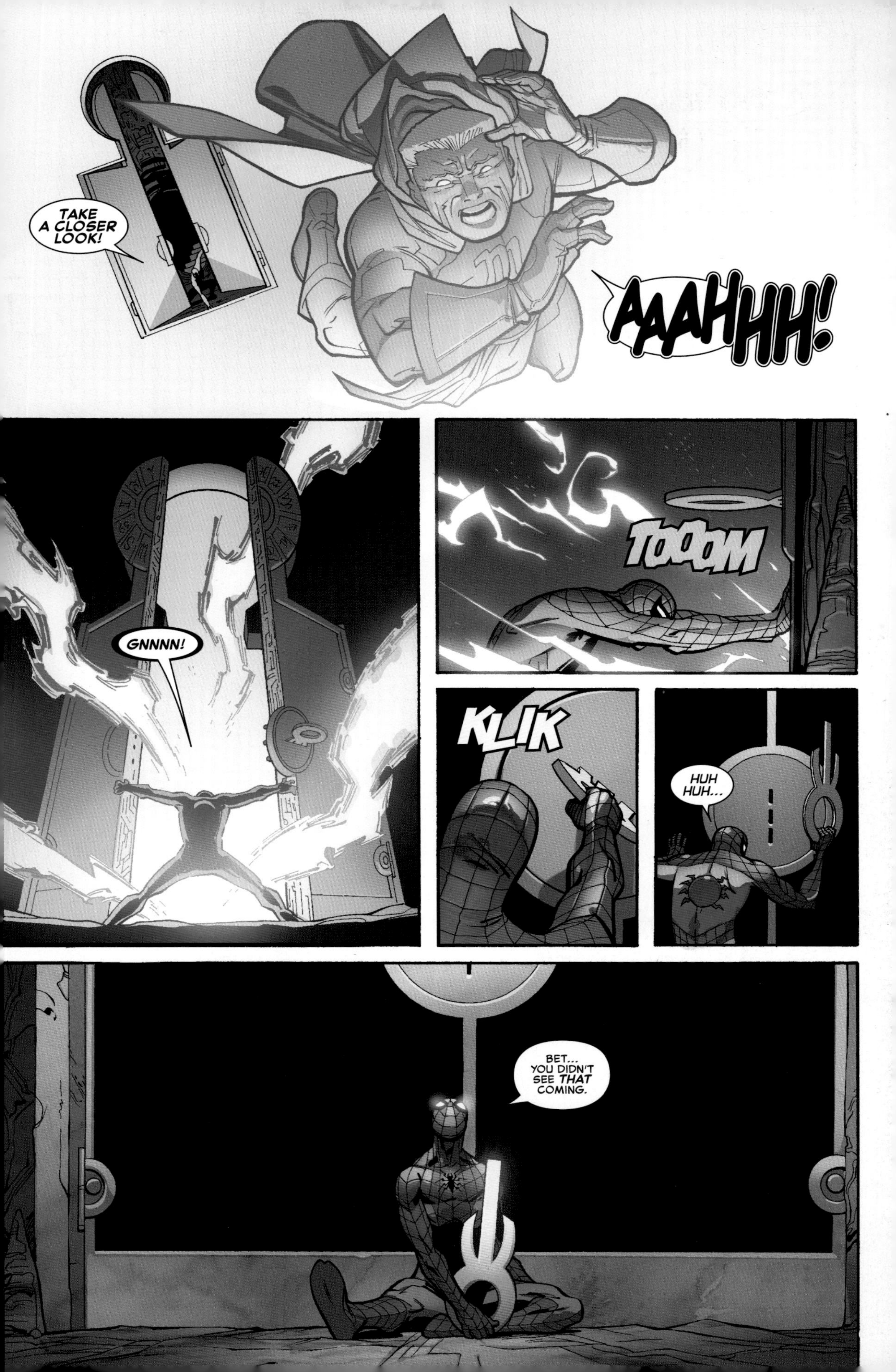
TAKE A CLOSER LOOK!
AAAHHH!
GNNNN!
TOOOM
KLIK
HUH HUH...
BET... YOU DIDN'T SEE *THAT* COMING.

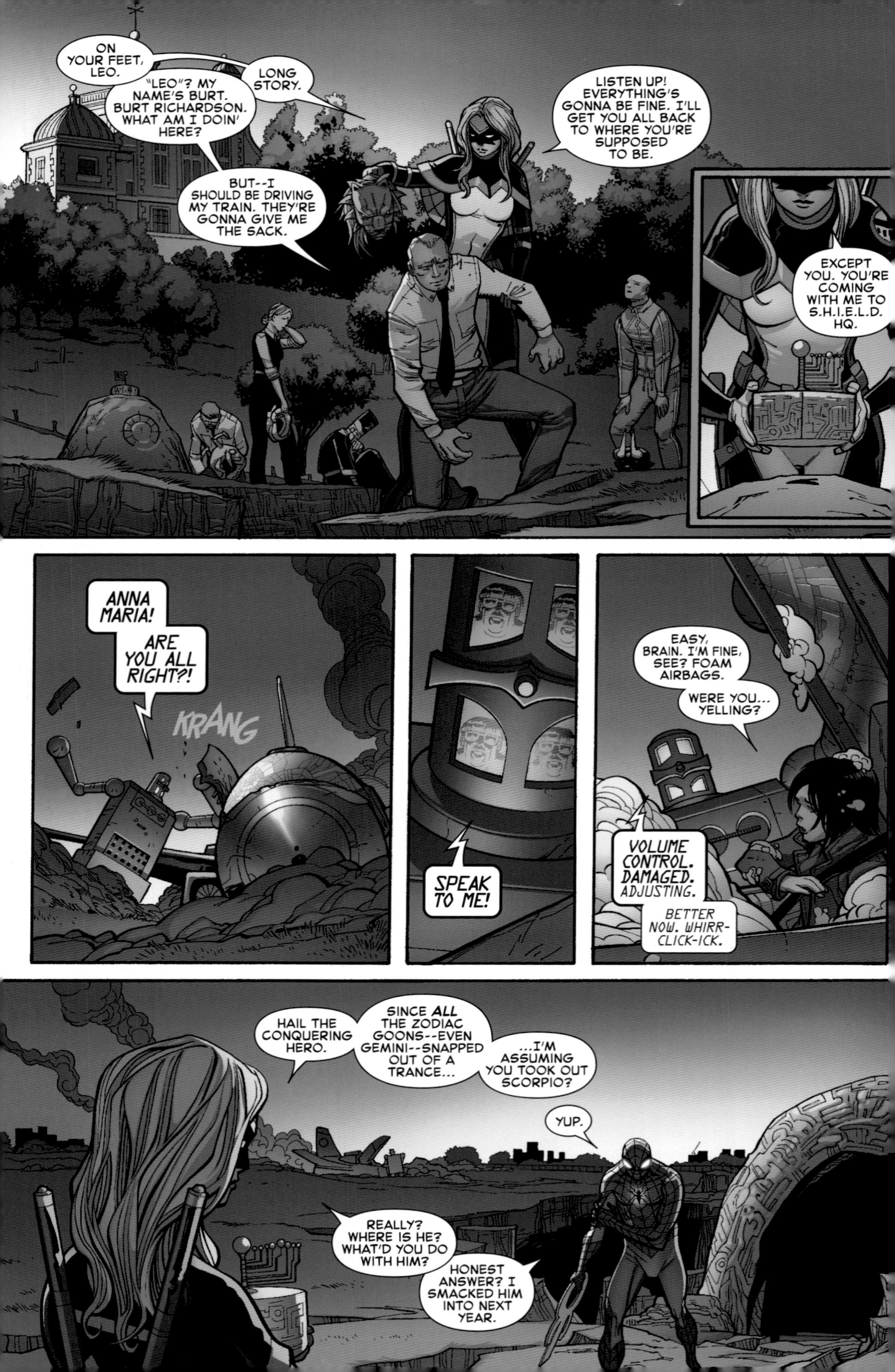
ON YOUR FEET, LEO.
LONG STORY.
"LEO"? MY NAME'S BURT. BURT RICHARDSON. WHAT AM I DOIN' HERE?
BUT--I SHOULD BE DRIVING MY TRAIN. THEY'RE GONNA GIVE ME THE SACK.
LISTEN UP! EVERYTHING'S GONNA BE FINE. I'LL GET YOU ALL BACK TO WHERE YOU'RE SUPPOSED TO BE.
EXCEPT YOU. YOU'RE COMING WITH ME TO S.H.I.E.L.D. HQ.
ANNA MARIA!
ARE YOU ALL RIGHT?!
KRANG
SPEAK TO ME!
EASY, BRAIN. I'M FINE, SEE? FOAM AIRBAGS.
WERE YOU... YELLING?
VOLUME CONTROL. DAMAGED. ADJUSTING.
BETTER NOW. WHIRR-CLICK-ICK.
HAIL THE CONQUERING HERO.
SINCE ALL THE ZODIAC GOONS--EVEN GEMINI--SNAPPED OUT OF A TRANCE...
...I'M ASSUMING YOU TOOK OUT SCORPIO?
YUP.
REALLY? WHERE IS HE? WHAT'D YOU DO WITH HIM?
HONEST ANSWER? I SMACKED HIM INTO NEXT YEAR.

The end...?

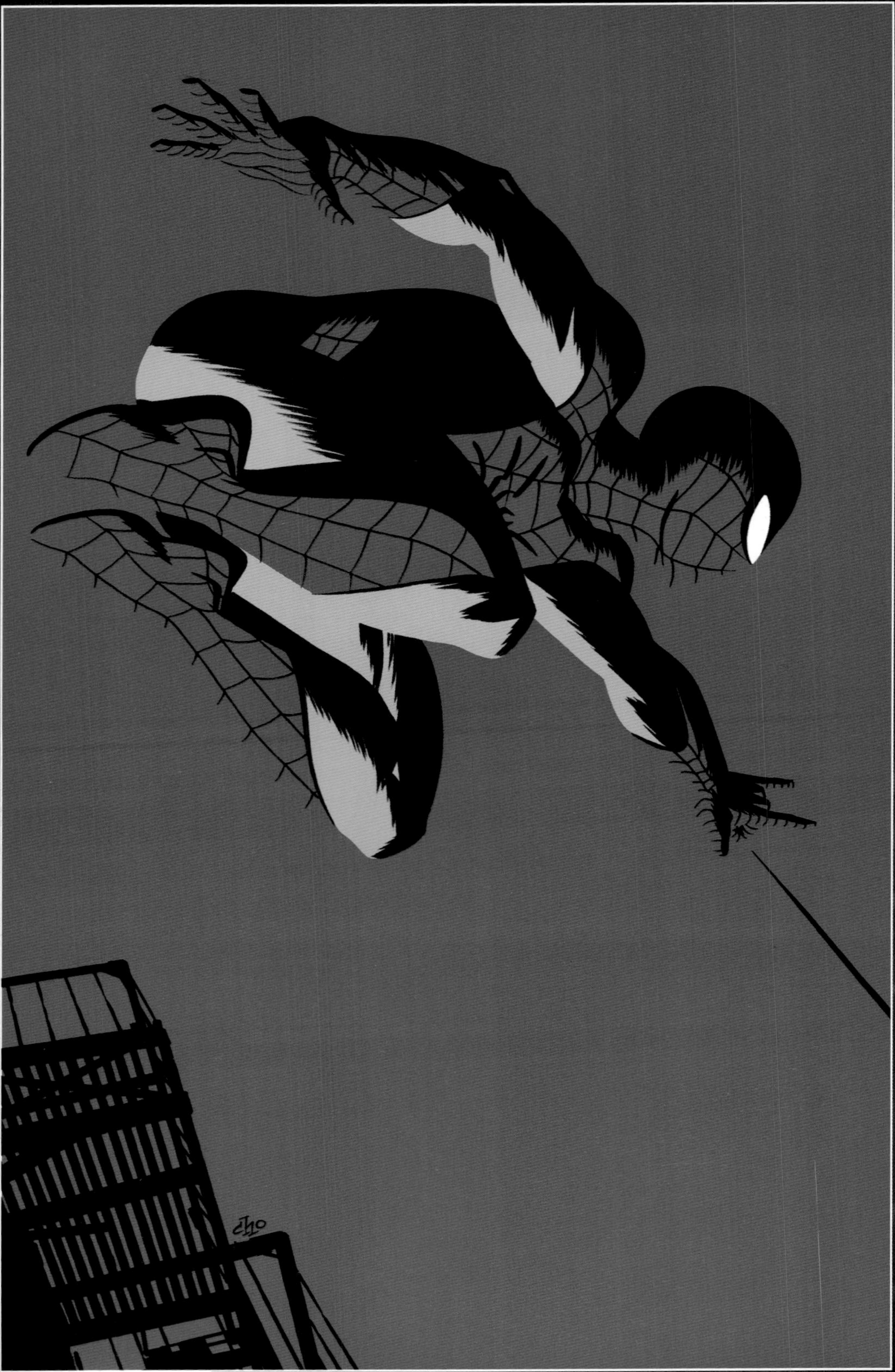
cho

Amazing Spider-Man #7
by Michael Cho

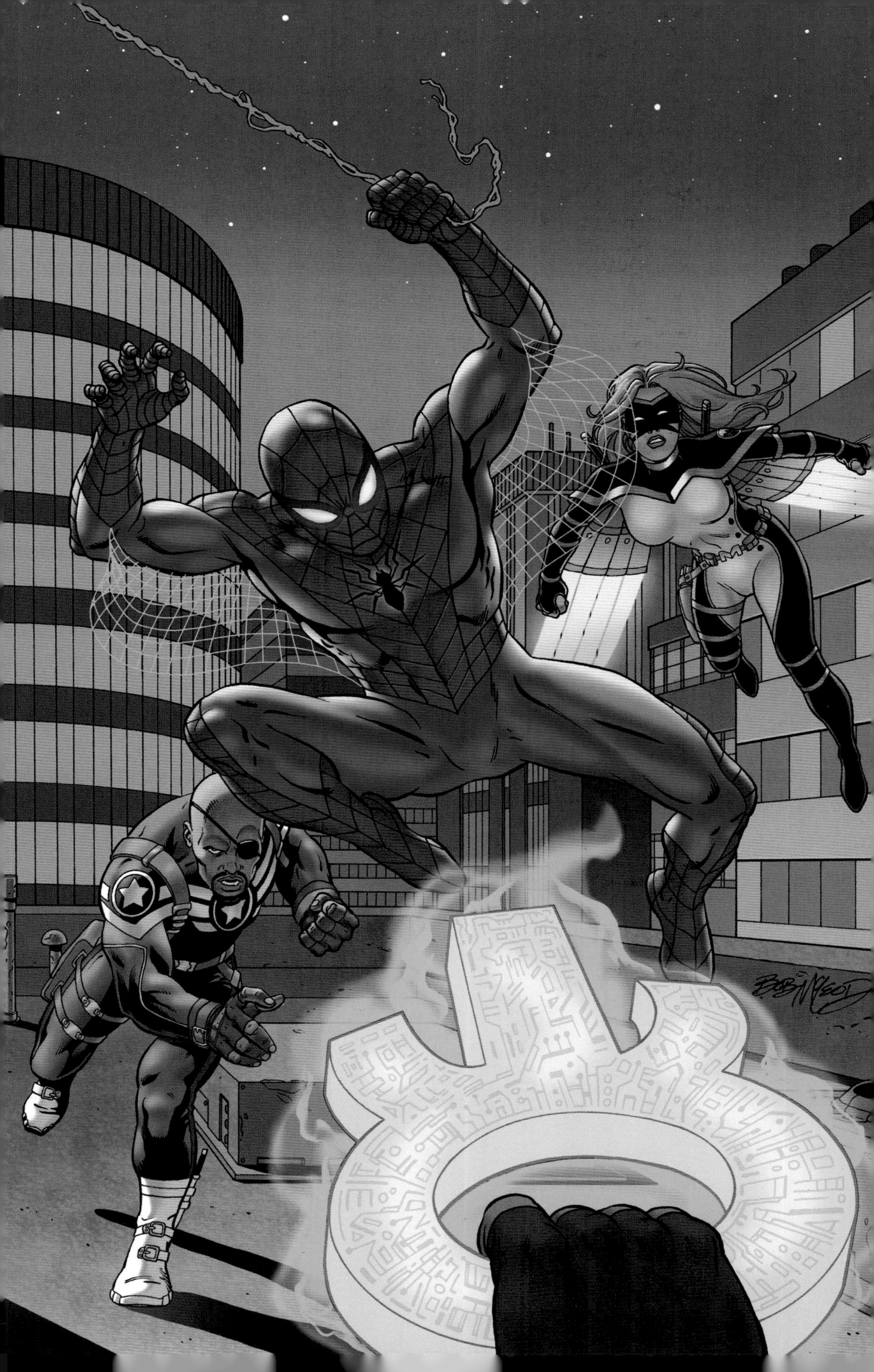

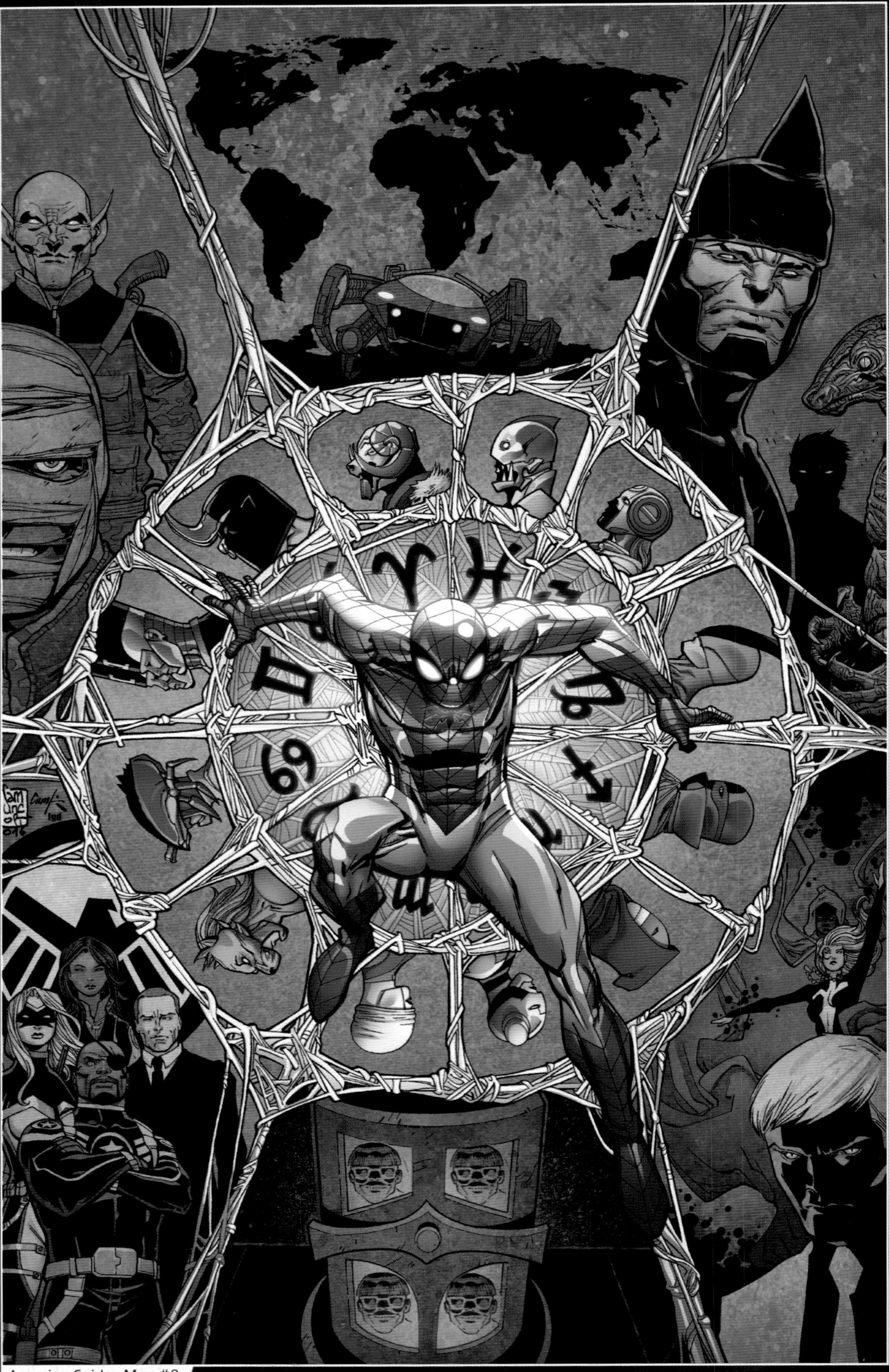

Amazing Spider-Man #9
by Giuseppe Camuncoli

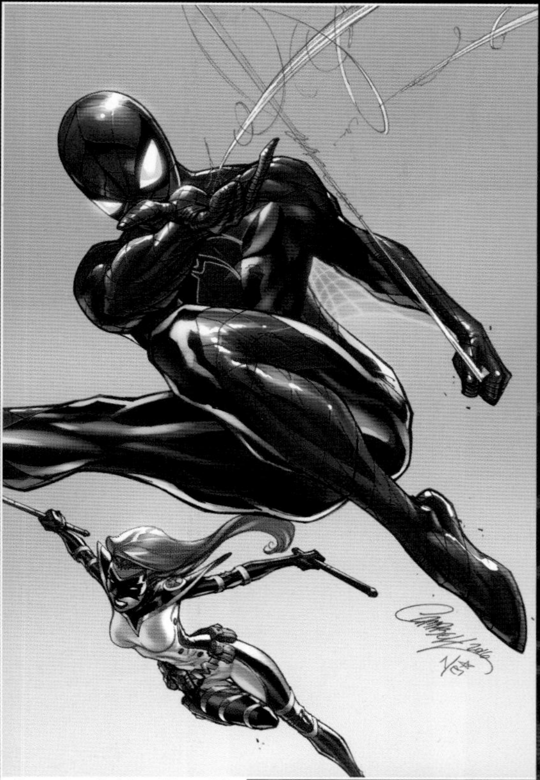

Amazing Spider-Man #9
by J Scott Campbell

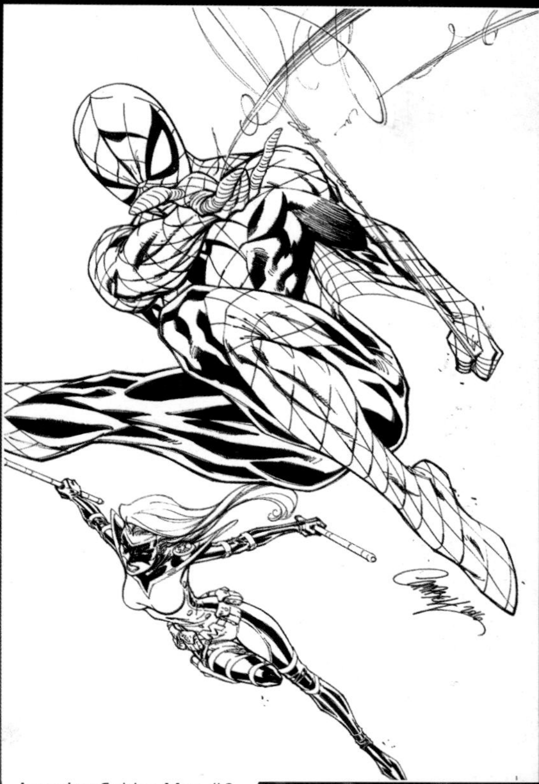

Amazing Spider-Man #9
by J Scott Campbell

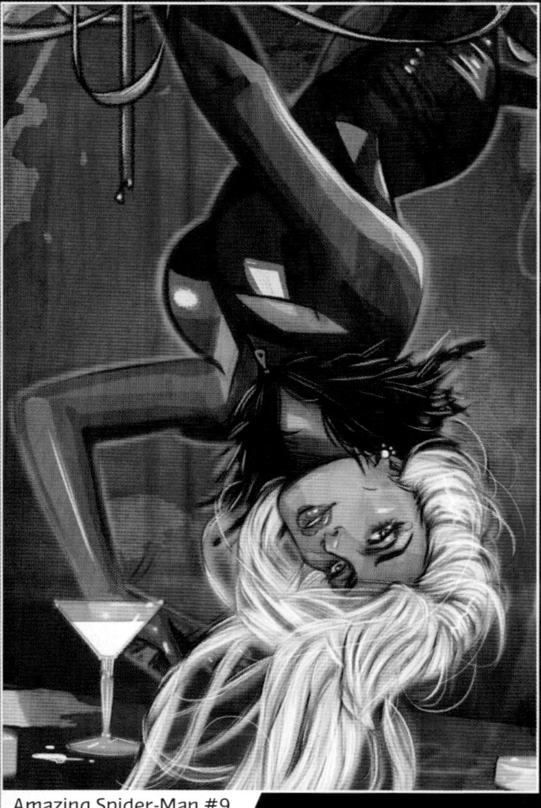

Amazing Spider-Man #9
by Tula Lotay

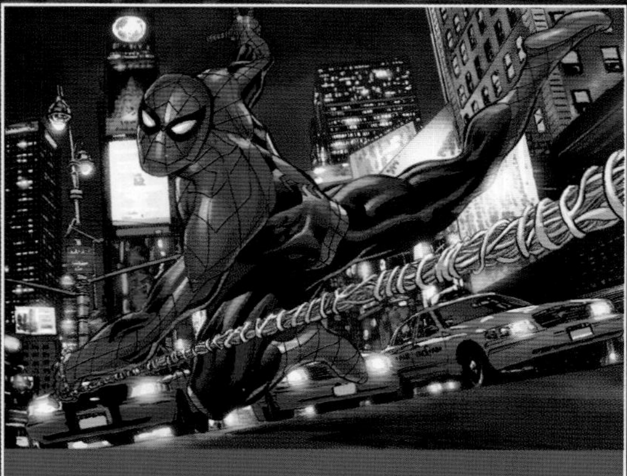

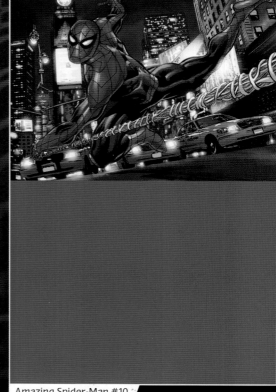

Amazing Spider-Man #10
by Mike Perkins

MARVEL™ PLATINUM
THE DEFINITIVE COLLECTION

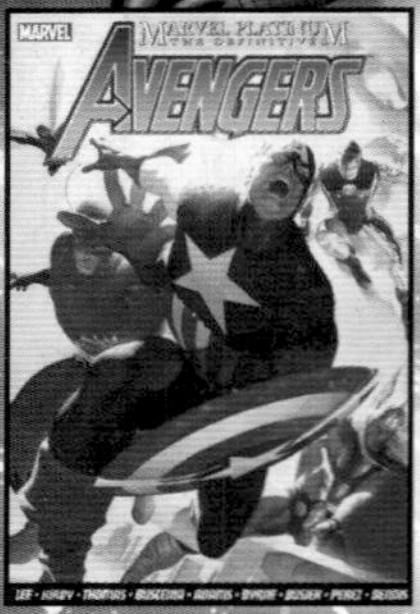

MARVEL
MARVEL PLATINUM
AVENGERS

Marvel Platinum:
The Definitive Avengers
ISBN: 978-1-84653-507-9
Pages: 308 **Price: £16.99**

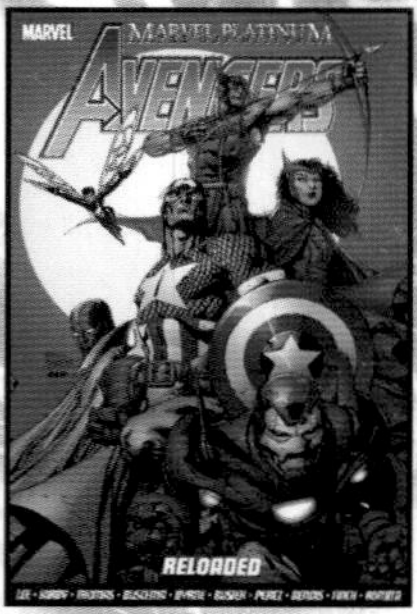

MARVEL
MARVEL PLATINUM
AVENGERS
RELOADED

Marvel Platinum:
The Definitive Avengers Reloaded
ISBN: 978-1-84653-643-4
Pages: 304 **Price: £16.99**

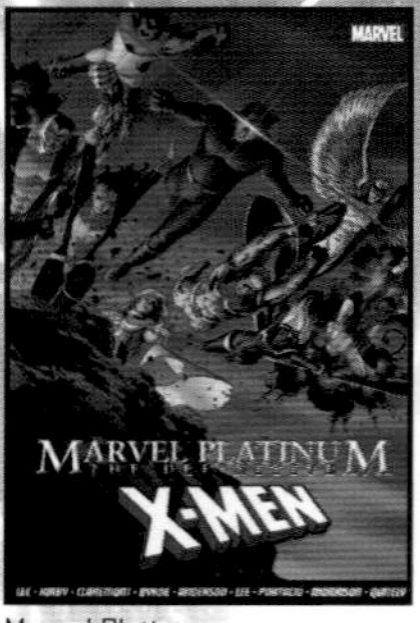

MARVEL
MARVEL PLATINUM
X-MEN

Marvel Platinum:
The Definitive X-Men
ISBN: 978-1-84653-599-4
Pages: 324 **Price: £16.99**

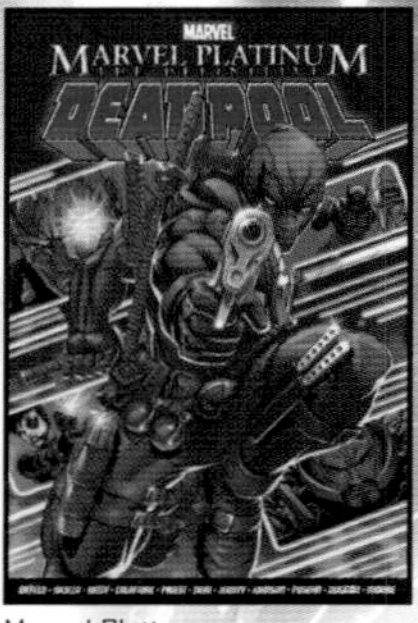

MARVEL
MARVEL PLATINUM
DEADPOOL

Marvel Platinum:
The Definitive Deadpool
ISBN: 978-1-84653-699-1
Pages: 316 **Price: £16.99**

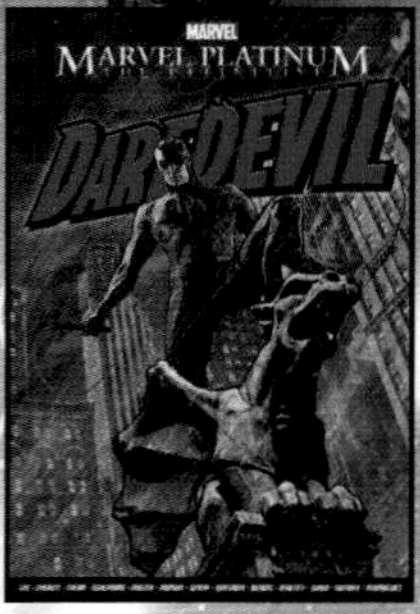

MARVEL
MARVEL PLATINUM
DAREDEVIL

Marvel Platinum:
The Definitive Daredevil
ISBN: 978-1-84653-704-2
Pages: 300 **Price: £16.99**

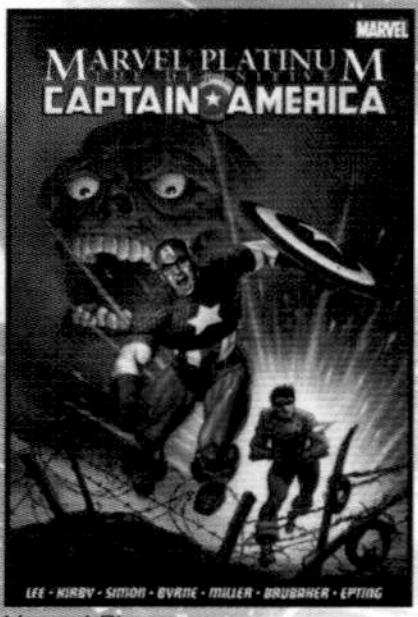

MARVEL
MARVEL PLATINUM
CAPTAIN AMERICA

Marvel Platinum:
The Definitive Captain America
ISBN: 978-1-84653-483-6
Pages: 296
Price: £15.99

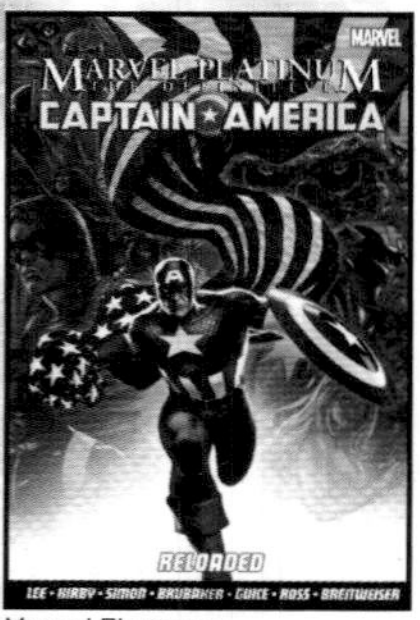

MARVEL
MARVEL PLATINUM
CAPTAIN AMERICA
RELOADED

Marvel Platinum:
The Definitive Captain America Reloaded
ISBN: 978-1-84653-580-2
Pages: 296 **Price: £16.99**

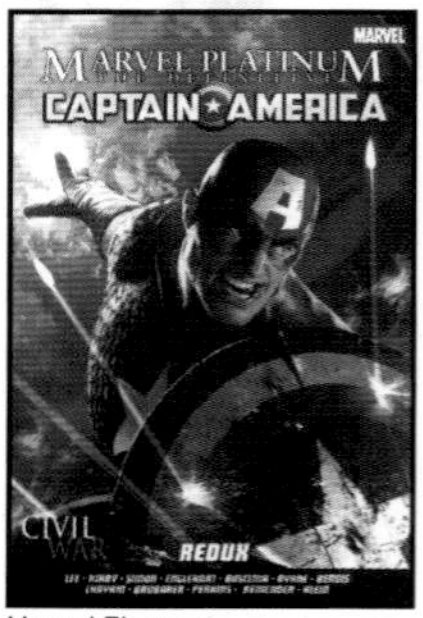

MARVEL
MARVEL PLATINUM
CAPTAIN AMERICA
CIVIL WAR
REDUX

Marvel Platinum:
The Definitive Captain America Redux
ISBN: 978-1-84653-726-4
Pages: 308 **Price: £16.99**

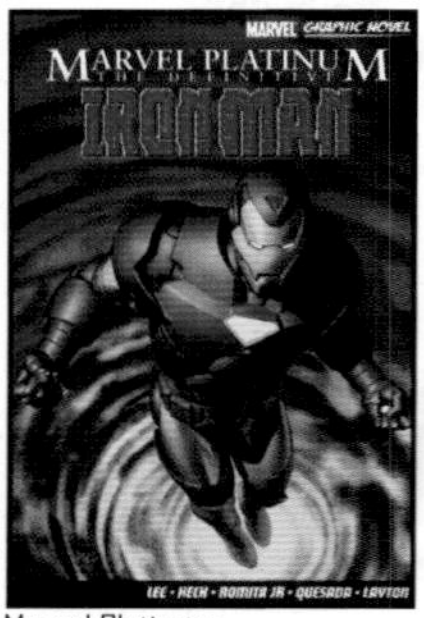

MARVEL GRAPHIC NOVEL
MARVEL PLATINUM
IRON MAN

Marvel Platinum:
The Definitive Iron Man
ISBN: 978-1-905239-85-6
Pages: 296
Price: £14.99

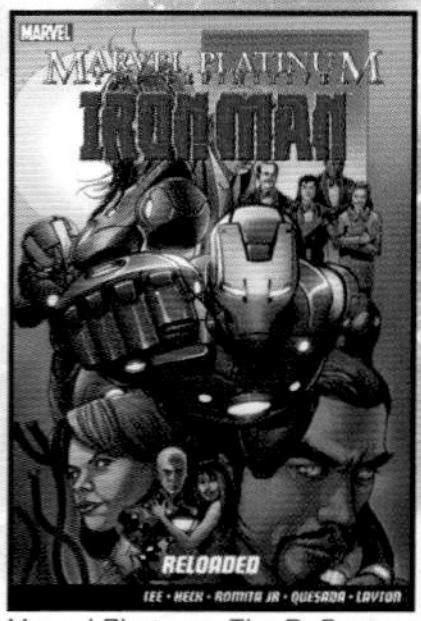

MARVEL
MARVEL PLATINUM
IRON MAN
RELOADED

Marvel Platinum: The Definitive Iron Man Reloaded
ISBN: 978-1-84653-529-1
Pages: 296
Price: £16.99

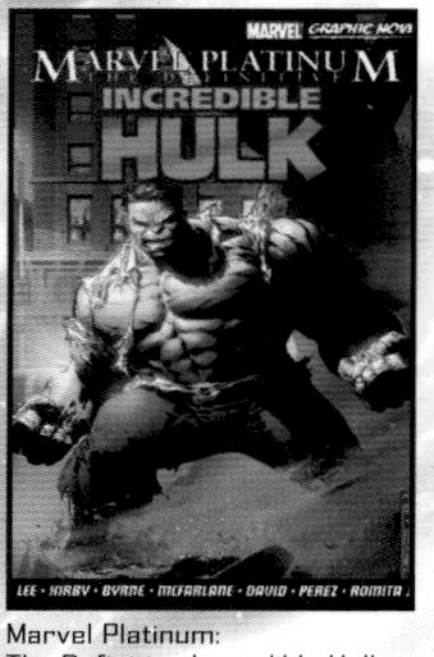

MARVEL GRAPHIC NOVEL
MARVEL PLATINUM
INCREDIBLE HULK

Marvel Platinum:
The Definitive Incredible Hulk
ISBN: 978-1-905239-88-7
Pages: 324 **Price: £14.99**

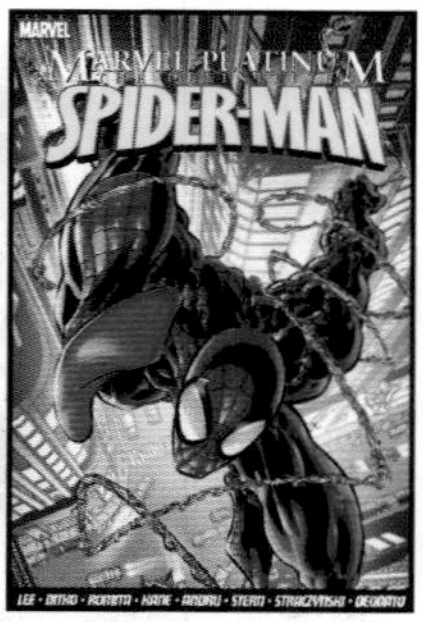

MARVEL
MARVEL PLATINUM
SPIDER-MAN

Marvel Platinum:
The Definitive Spider-Man
ISBN: 978-1-84653-510-9
Pages: 296 **Price: £15.99**

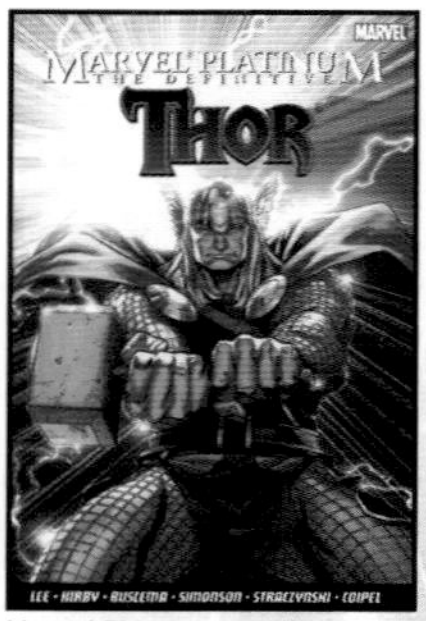

MARVEL
MARVEL PLATINUM
THOR

Marvel Platinum:
The Definitive Thor
ISBN: 978-1-84653-481-2
Pages: 296 **Price: £15.99**

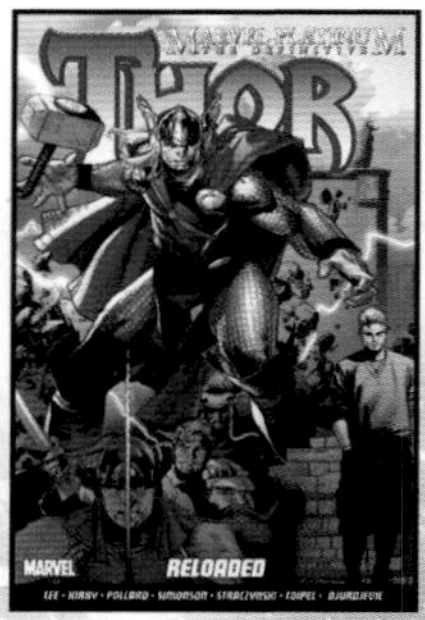

MARVEL PLATINUM
THOR
MARVEL
RELOADED

Marvel Platinum:
The Definitive Thor Reloaded
ISBN: 978-1-84653-552-9
Pages: 300 **Price: £16.99**

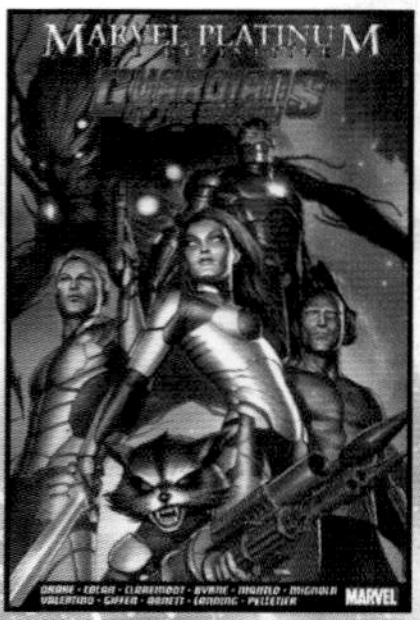

MARVEL PLATINUM
MARVEL

Marvel Platinum: The Definitive Guardians of the Galaxy
ISBN: 978-1-84653-601-4
Pages: 336 **Price: £16.99**

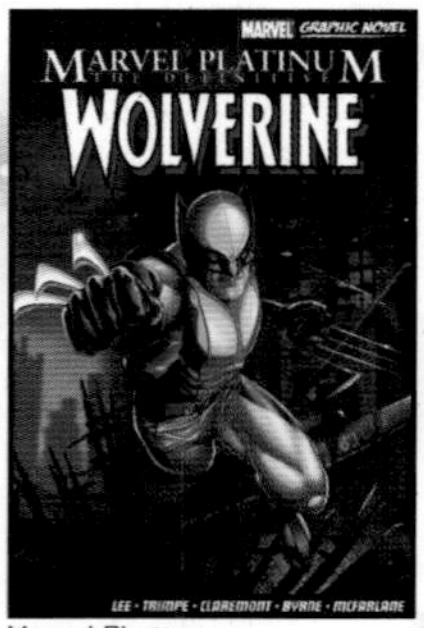

MARVEL GRAPHIC NOVEL
MARVEL PLATINUM
WOLVERINE

Marvel Platinum:
The Definitive Wolverine
ISBN: 978-1-84653-409-6
Pages: 356 **Price: £16.99**

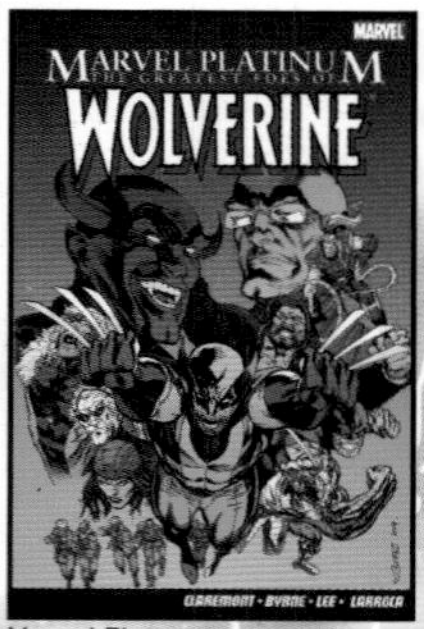

MARVEL
MARVEL PLATINUM
WOLVERINE

Marvel Platinum:
The Greatest Foes of Wolverine
ISBN: 978-1-84653-422-5
Pages: 372 **Price: £16.99**

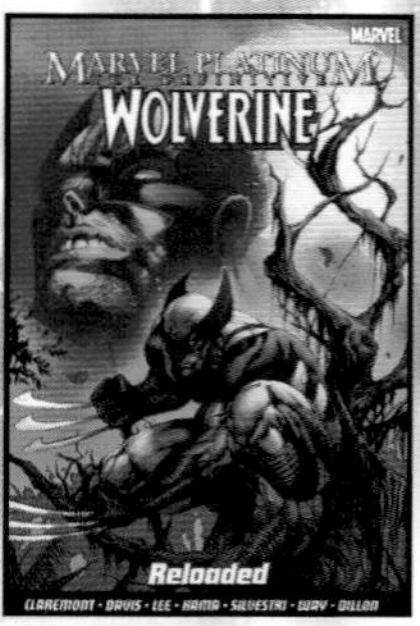

MARVEL
MARVEL PLATINUM
WOLVERINE
Reloaded

Marvel Platinum: The Definitive Wolverine Reloaded
ISBN: 978-1-84653-537-6
Pages: 296 **Price: £16.99**

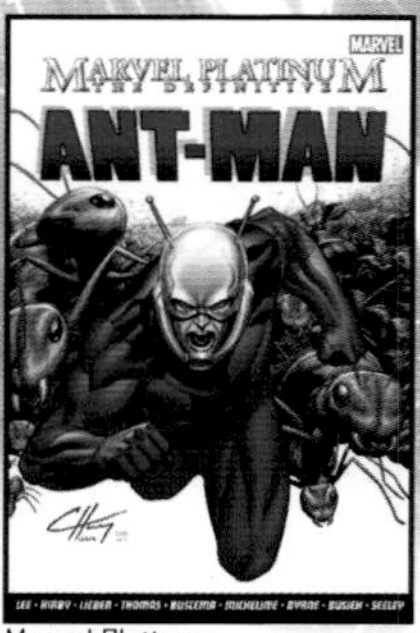

MARVEL
MARVEL PLATINUM
ANT-MAN

Marvel Platinum:
The Definitive Ant-Man
ISBN: 978-1-84653-658-8
Pages: 320 **Price: £16.99**

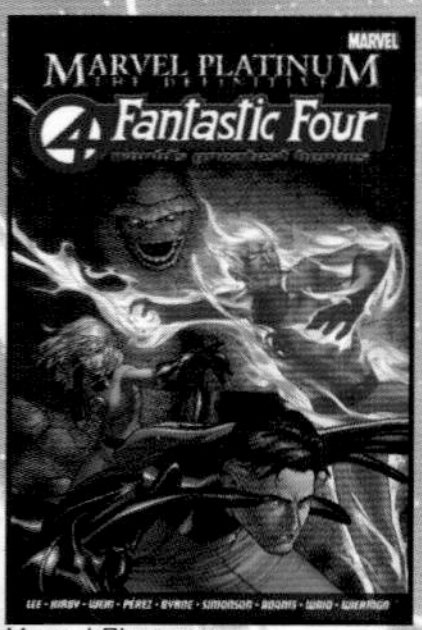

MARVEL
MARVEL PLATINUM
Fantastic Four

Marvel Platinum:
The Definitive Fantastic Four
ISBN: 978-1-84653-654-0
Pages: 296 **Price: £16.99**

AVAILABLE FROM ALL GOOD BOOKSTORES, COMICSHOPS AND ONLINE RETAILERS!